A.G.

5 EASY STEPS TO ENDING A TOXIC RELATIONSHIP

Unplug the Negativity Cord and Jump-Start Your Emotional Healing

Book Design: Felix Barca

Book Cover: Felix Barca

ISBN: 9781695657946

Published in the United States.

Table of Contents

How I Stopped Being a
"Toxic Relationships" Addict

It happened before I learned how to dance salsa. Before I traveled to Abadiania to see John of God in flesh and blood. Before I moved to California, the land of blue skies and open hearts. Before that, I was a "toxic relationships" addict. Not knowing that I was one made things even worse.

It all started a few months after I turned 21. I was still living—with a hole in my soul and an insatiable hunger for love—in Bucharest, Romania, the city where I was born on the same day *Star Wars* made its debut on the big screens in the US.

At first, the loss of my father to a sudden heart attack didn't seem to affect me much. I shed few tears over the event, didn't wear black (the way you're supposed to when a close relative passes away), and shot the video presentations for my weekly music show on the rooftop of one of the tallest buildings in the city. I loved being a TV host and producer, and nothing could stop me from doing it—not even the death of my own father.

Looking back, I realize that I had built high and thick walls to keep the pain away. They were disguised as the need to stay strong for my mom; freedom from my father's authoritative and demanding dominion; and a focus on my TV career and academic studies.

The truth is, I had no idea who I was or what I wanted in life. Music made me happy. Being in front of the camera or asked for an autograph in the street made me happy. Having a boyfriend made me happy, at least for a while.

Eugene made me happy at first. I had met him at 16. He was already an established musician, ranking yearly among the best and sexiest guitar players, and he drove a fancy car. However, it wasn't until after my father passed away that I became his girlfriend.

He asked me to lunch and, by the time we were done, he said, "I've been attracted to you for years, and we look so cute together. I think we should start dating."

He was recently divorced and I was newly single.

I hated being single and he was very much my type of man—
dark eyes, dark hair, lean body, an artist, well-spoken, well-
traveled, experienced. An impressive number of women were
throwing themselves at him all the time ... and he was choosing
me.

I said, "Yes."

A month later, I moved into his apartment, away from my
neighborhood and the city center, the TV studios, and the
university where I was earning my Bachelor of Arts degree in
Foreign Languages and Literatures. But hey, who cared? I was
the girlfriend of a rock star. I accompanied him to his concerts.
I got to sit at the band's table and was the recipient of envious
looks from the women in the audience. Whenever I could, I
traveled with him across the country.

I paid little attention to the details. My clothes were stacked in
a small closet, piled up against a couple of cardboard boxes, a
broom, and a vacuum cleaner. They wouldn't have fit in the
large mahogany wardrobe in Eugene's bedroom. He
continuously praised his ex-wife's qualities and talked about
how the apartment had looked so much tidier when she had
lived there. He made sure his mother visited him when I was at
work or in class. He never gave me a word of praise or
appreciation. I don't think he ever told me, "I love you."

A few months into our relationship, the butterflies in my
stomach lost their wings and the big smile on face faded away.

The more distant and critical my boyfriend became, the more bitter I grew. A voice in my head whispered to me that he didn't love and respect me.

The more I heard that voice, the more I craved his love and attention. I wanted things to be as they had been at the beginning. I wanted to prove that my father had been wrong when he had said I was stupid with men.

I knew Eugene still desired me, so I played the card of fulfilling his sexual needs even when I didn't feel like it. I also tried to cook, though I didn't know how. My efforts paid off for short periods of time. Eugene would kiss me and hug me and be kind; he would make me feel valued and worthy. For a few hours or even days, I would be on cloud nine only to find myself back in a dark place as soon as he behaved as though I didn't exist.

I was on an emotional rollercoaster and my humor shifted according to his behavior. One day, it was at the highest high. The next day, it had plummeted to the lowest low. My relationship was the only thing that really mattered. It was like driving around in a car. Eugene, his words and actions, sat in the driver's seat while my mom, still in shock, my friends, my career, and my studies were locked inside the trunk.

I had no idea how to handle the situation, as I had never experienced these kinds of ups and downs before. Bottom line,

I had never been in a toxic relationship before.

According to psychologists, a toxic relationship is one that is unfavorable to you or others. In my opinion, a challenging relationship becomes toxic once it stops serving its purpose. This type of interaction is characterized by insecurity, self-centeredness, dominance, and control. It can take a toll on your career, health, finances, and social life. It usually undermines the core values of a healthy personality such as self-confidence, self-worth, self-esteem, self-love, and assertiveness.

Although a big scarlet letter lies upon toxic relationships, they carry a buried treasure. Sometimes, we must hit rock bottom before we can find our inner strength, our gifts and talents. Sometimes, we must become aware that we are playing the victim role so that we decide we don't want to be one anymore.

When we see the abusive partner as a teacher who is there to help us evolve, a toxic relationship becomes a massive opportunity for growth. We can't change other people, but we can change ourselves. As we do, the whole world and the people in it change, too.

My relationship with Eugene lasted only a few months. One day, I put all my clothes in the trunk of my car and left. By then, I had met another man who made me feel beautiful, desired, attractive, and worthy.

Another toxic relationship followed and then another, full of adrenaline and drama. Believe it or not, although they caused me pain, these relationships also made me feel alive and gave me a purpose to live for when nothing else did.

Eventually, I realized I was walking in circles, repeating the same story and patterns with different men. That's when I stopped complaining about how all the good men were taken and started looking for answers within myself.

I've been on this journey for 10 years now, and I still can't see the "end" sign. It has been a journey of healing, self-love, deeper awareness, self-acceptance, self-discovery, synchronicities, miracles, faith, and discovering and embracing my life purpose. However, it has also been a journey of despair, disappointment, sadness, and lack of trust.

With each tear and burst of anger, I shed an illusion about myself. With each miracle and wish come true, I embraced my role as a conscious creator of my life.

As toxicity cleared out of my inner landscape, my couple relationship became less toxic until, finally, I met a man with whom I rise in love (instead of falling in love).

You don't have to be in a toxic relationship. You don't have to accept a life situation that puts you down, prevents you from fulfilling your dreams, and doesn't honor you. There are no excuses for that. You have the power to say no, to move forward, to transform. You deserve to be loved, to be happy, to thrive. You are beautiful and amazing.

I hope this book will be your friend and ally on your journey toward freeing yourself from what no longer serves you and finding the true love that's meant for you.

The Ill-Fated Tomato and Other Warning Signs of a Toxic Relationship

The second he opened the lid of the fridge door top side-pocket, I had a bad feeling.

The half-tomato slipped from where I had put it after breakfast. Before he could catch it, the tomato had painted the cream-colored floor tiles with juicy red dots.

His eyes bulged and his voice thundered.

"What's so complicated about properly storing a tomato in the fridge? A kid can do it. Why can't you? Now I've lost my appetite because of you!"

"But...." I whispered, looking away.

The thud of the living room door silenced my voice. I decided to clean up the mess before following him to the patio and trying to regain his good graces.

As I kneeled by the ill-fated tomato, I wished I were somebody else. I wished I were one of those women whom men respect and adore. I wished I could have smiled and joked and cupped his face as a wise mother would do with her belligerent child. But how could I have done that? My lover's words had made my self-esteem plummet to zero. Guilt had replaced joy. His anger had made my heart race with fear.

My boyfriend was right. In that very moment, I was no longer a grown-up woman. Rather, I was a little girl terrified of losing the love and acceptance of the most important man in her life—the man she loved. I was someone permanently living on the edge of her seat and walking on eggshells to keep alive an already dead and dysfunctional relationship, just because she believed she had found the man of her dreams. Of course, things weren't always sour. We also had fantastic chemistry.

It's hard to be objective and make the best decisions when we're in love, isn't it? Or when we lose ourselves, forget who we are, and live in fear. We have so many blind spots that we don't realize what's going on, that the other person is trying to control us no matter what.

In a healthy relationship, both partners have equal control. They feel free to express their feelings and emotions and to say "no." They know that though they may sometimes disagree, they respect and love each other. They uplift, inspire, and support each other.

In a toxic relationship, one of the partners must be in control and have all the power all the time. I don't necessarily mean physical violence or substance abuse. If this is the case, find a safe place, pack your bags, leave, or ask for help, and then continue reading this book.

Power and control can manifest in more subtle ways.

The person may act deliberately upon that need, or not be aware. However, the effects are the same. The other person in the relationship feels as though they are on an emotional rollercoaster.

Anger and **guilt**, like in the above story, are two of the most common control methods in a toxic relationship. Also, a small incident can be blown out of proportions.

Anger or a **bad temper** is accompanied by withdrawal. In the days after "the falling of the tomato," there was a total lack of meaningful interaction. He barely talked to me and refused to come anywhere near me, as if I had the plague.

Ensuring that every item in the fridge was securely stored didn't prevent similar scenes later. What I said or how I said it, or even my driving style, could lead to a sudden outburst of anger, like a storm on a summer day. My ability to focus on my professional projects dropped alarmingly and I lost weight. I started to act guarded and closed up out of fear that, at any given moment, something I said or did would send him into a rage. I secretly wished that his friends and the people who liked him for being such a pleasant and easygoing man would know about his offensive side and his inability to take responsibility for his actions and emotions.

But that's what a toxic partner does: blames the other and triggers guilt.

According to David Hawkins, **guilt** is one of the lowest vibrations a human being can experience. It is lower than fear and anger. When we feel guilty, we are easy to manipulate and control because we want to redeem ourselves and feel worthy again. A toxic partner shows no compassion and tolerance. They find ways to make their partner feel guilty every time the partner fails to do what they want.

If you think that's it ... wait! The game is more complicated than that. "Removing guilt"—but only when you humor or please your partner— is an essential part of it. Beware of this tool, especially if you're a guilt-prone individual, anything or anyone who removes guilt is attractive and potentially addictive.

Guilt-induction manifests not only in couple relationships but also between friends and family members. Unfortunately, some parents still use guilt-induction to "educate" their children. More about this topic later in the book.

*

*　　*

Maria, a dear friend of mine, an adorable woman in her early 30s, had recently broken up with her boyfriend after almost two years of trying to make things work.

They matched up on one of the popular dating apps and started seeing each other. My friend, an independent woman and successful professional in her field, didn't care much about his struggle with finances or his recent divorce. All she needed was a man who loved her and wanted to be with her. In the beginning, that's who he was.

This man brought her flowers and took her out. They shared long walks and dinners and laughter. He made sweet love to her and held her tightly during the long winter nights.

But once they moved in together, he started complaining about his finances and about how his employers were wronging him. He let her make decisions only to pout later at her choices. He also told her that he liked slim women; he said that she was too fat and should lose weight immediately. If she didn't, he would break up with her.

Do you recognize yourself in this situation?

If you do, know that **over-dependency** and **belittling** are tools that a toxic partner uses to control you.

The partner can play the over-dependent role, letting you make all the decisions only to make you feel bad about yourself later by displaying a passive-aggressive behavior.

In a healthy relationship, the partners speak openly about their likes and dislikes. A toxic partner likes to see you bang your head against a brick wall and won't tell what caused them discomfort.

Belittling is one of the most potent manipulation tools. That's because, in our heads, we already have a negative voice that constantly criticizes us. Over time, this combination can dramatically reduce our self-esteem, self-worth, and self-value, and build a distorted picture of ourselves in our minds.

When we feel as though we're not good enough, we act like beggars. We believe we don't have options and we are happy with anything others throw at us. We become dependent on them.

A toxic partner will not hesitate to make fun of or criticize his spouse or girlfriend in public. Often, he'll pretend it's a joke. His goal is to make you doubt your ability to make decisions and to convince you that nobody else will find you attractive and interesting.

*
*   *

The day had been terribly awful. It was like one of those days when you get up on the wrong side of the bed. One mishap triggers another and your spirit sinks below the ocean level.

It happened back in the days when I was a TV host. The station where I worked was a sinking ship. If I wanted to pursue this career, I had to find new opportunities. A friend had told me about a sports news anchor position with a burgeoning channel. I went for a screen test and passed it with flying colors. They sent me into the field to cover a soccer game as a reporter. They were happy with the result and made me an offer.

The morning of the big day, my boyfriend was still pouting because of an argument we'd had the previous evening. I decided to ignore it and simply focus on what I had to do. I entered the program manager's office with a big smile on my face and my lucky pen at hand in my purse. The meeting lasted only a few minutes—the necessary amount of time to apologize and say the job was no longer on the table because they had decided to restructure the news department.

I left the building in tears and swore that I'd give up being a TV host. At first, my boyfriend was supportive. He took me out to lunch and held my hand. However, beyond his words of encouragement and pledges of support, I sensed a sort of aloofness that silenced me. So many thoughts and feeling were running wild in my mind, yet I found myself unable to voice them.

Minutes after we parted ways, my boyfriend called me.

"I feel I'm making you miserable. I just needed to tell you that. Talk to you later. Bye."

Yes, that's what he did. As if I didn't already have to deal with my own stuff, now I had to deal with his, too. That doesn't happen in healthy relationships, but it's ordinary in toxic relationships.

The toxic partner isn't empathetic about your situation or feelings. In particular, when you try to communicate about how their behavior and words hurt or make you uncomfortable, they overreact or deflect it on you. You end up taking care of their unhappiness and anger. You comfort them instead of receiving comfort yourself. Their fault becomes your fault. It's your fault that they act selfish, unloving, or disrespectful and don't keep their promises.

Partners can be toxic not only by doing something but also by not doing something. To feel safe and secure, we all need solid ground beneath our feet. A toxic partner will never give you that. They will play "the independent:" say that nobody can control them, often break their promises, keep you guessing, make you do what they want you to do to get them to commit to you.

Though your efforts and patience pay off every now and then, in the long run, this game is a losing one—for you!

*

* *

I had no idea who came up with the idea that jealousy and possessiveness represent signs of love, but I find it totally twisted.

Horea is one of the finest guitar players in Romania and an exceptional human being. Charismatic and talented, he always draws the most beautiful women. I remember years ago, when he was playing in Bucharest and his gorgeous girlfriend remained in Timisoara, their hometown, we had a long conversation about music, creativity, and relationships.

He confessed that his girlfriend was puzzled because he was not jealous about the many admirers trying to win her over.

"I told her love is freedom," he said. "She's free as a bird to spread her wings and fly. I know that if she loves me, she'll stay."

With love, it's this simple: no strings, no restrictions, no boundaries. Just trust, magic, and unfolding.

Try to explain this concept to a possessive, controlling partner.

Although their mellow outbursts of jealousy may flatter you at first ("Yes, yes, yes! Somebody finally WANTS me!"), they end up eating away at your wellbeing as you progress into the relationship. As time passes, this type of toxic partner becomes more controlling and suspicious. They question every action and word and they violate your privacy by breaking into your social media accounts and checking your phone. Even worse, they do all they can to eliminate any meaningful relationships in your life.

If you allow them, these people will end up possessing you and robbing you of your life.

It's never too late to break free, but it's better to not get in that situation.

Paying attention to the red flags and not rushing into a relationship will save you time, early gray hairs, and tears.

Most men are extremely nice and generous when they are courting a woman. They will go out of their way to please her, support her, and make her feel like a queen. Only time will tell if this is a strategy or if he's genuinely interested you and your happiness.

A loving partner doesn't need constant praise or returned favors. The twinkle in your eyes, your wellbeing, and your joy are his rewards.

A toxic partner has an agenda. Those small acts of service and little gifts aren't for you, but for them, so they can feel generous and also be entitled to get at least the same from you.

If only they'd appreciate it! Unfortunately, they won't. You can bend over backward to please them, but you will always end up never doing enough for them. When you dare to object to one of their requests or when you can't offer help, they make a fuss over what they've done for you. They try to induce guilt.

I call this type of toxic partner "the accountant" (with apologies to members of this profession) because they treat the relationship like a balance sheet. The credit column must display bigger numbers than the debit one.

If, at some point, they find someone willing to do more for them, they break up with you without any remorse.

*

*　　*

Control and abuse constitute one way of looking at toxic relationships. But it's like looking at a glass and seeing only its empty half.

The expression itself casts the people involved in the specific roles of "victim" and "aggressor." It also casts a stigma on their interaction.

After years of spiritual and metaphysical study and practice, I came to the realization that, often, we enter challenging relationships to grow. Our souls call for that particular experience because we need it.

We need a teacher to remind us to be loving, compassionate, forgiving, and kind.

We need a mirror in which we can see the aspects of ourselves that we reject.

We need a wake-up call for our healing process.

Our partners—the ones who push our buttons, poke at our sore wounds and make us feel worthless—give us all these gifts. According to ancient oriental wisdom, these people don't show up in our lives randomly. Contracts between our souls are agreed upon long before we start our human experience as human beings. The truth is, no matter how bleak the situation between two people is, we are here to help each other.

If you look at all your past relationships, you will discover a common thread, almost a pattern. That's because when we refuse or fail to learn the lesson, the situation will keep repeating. Your co-star may differ, but the scenario stays pretty much the same.

The relationship is fantastic in the beginning and becomes a battle scene months later. Your partner is crazy about you for a year, then falls in love with somebody else. Every partner cheats on you or lies to you. The list of examples can go on.

The toxicity in your relationship shows the level of toxicity in your relationship with yourself. According to the law of attraction, you get what you vibrate. When you lack self-confidence and self-worth, when you don't love and accept yourself, you end attracting partners who, eventually, will mirror that to you.

When you lie to other people, and especially to yourself, you end up attracting liars. When you overly criticize yourself, your partner will belittle you.

When you harbor limiting beliefs such "all men cheat" or "relationships are hard work," you draw those kinds of people and experiences into your reality.

The way out of a toxic relationship is to build a different relationship with yourself and the world, one based on love and acceptance.

Toxicity Checklist

Look at the list below and check the words that best describe the way you feel in your relationship. Write those words on a piece of paper and store it in a safe place. You'll need it later.

O Guilty	O Edgy
O Afraid	O Manipulated
O Unworthy	O Wronged
O Powerless	O Undervalued
O Drained	O Disrespected
O Lost	O Unloved
O Used	O Abused
O Unsafe	

Five Anchors You Need to Cut Loose Before Anything Will Get Better

I opened my eyes to an empty home. Less than half an hour ago, he had been standing in the doorjamb, looking at me in silence before leaving the room. I had thought he still had work to do, so I went on with my mindfulness routine.

By the time I was done, he was nowhere to be found. Not in his office, not in the living room or kitchen. He had just taken off without saying a word or leaving a note. My heart raced with anger. It felt so unfair. Earlier, he had told me he could feel my love for him all the time.

"Why would you act like that with a person who loves you and whom you pretend to love?"

His behavior didn't make any sense. Again!

My first impulse was to pack my stuff, take off, and never talk to him again. But I couldn't bring myself to do it. Instead, I called him to tell him I was leaving.

He kept his cool. Said he didn't want to disturb me during my spiritual practice and would be back soon. He said he'd rather have me wait for him to come back, but I was free to do as I pleased.

"Why do you hate me?" I asked.

"I don't hate you," he said in a neutral voice.

At the moment, hate seemed to be the only logical explanation for his attitude. Hate makes people deliberately inflict pain on other people.

While still on the phone, I got into my car and let the engine run for a few minutes. My soul kept telling me, "Leave now." Meanwhile, my foot couldn't release the brake pedal.

Part of me—the part that refused to accept that things didn't work between us and that clung to the image he had put forward during his courtship time—wanted to forgive him.

I waited for him to come back. We made up.

Becoming aware that you're in a toxic relationship is your first step to freedom. But even then, it can be so difficult to leave. Although your soul and intuition guide you to make the best decisions, you turn a deaf ear and allow heavy anchors to keep you stuck in an unhealthy situation. You ignore the long-term effects and focus on fulfilling a momentary need.

Fear is the most potent anchor that keeps people stuck in toxic relationships. People fear different things, such as not being good enough or adequate, solitude, and inner emptiness. They fear what other people will say. They fear poverty and financial limitations.

My friend Dana is one of those women. In her prime years, she always got what she wanted. She had a high-paying job and turned men's heads wherever she went. When she reached her mid-40s, her company downsized and let her go. No matter how hard she tried, she couldn't find proper employment. Many recruiters evaluated her as over-qualified. Others said they were looking for younger people. Dana had never failed before, so this situation dealt a heavy blow. Her couple relationship was no bed of roses, either. Although she had planned to break up with her boyfriend, she stayed in the relationship because of his financial support. Fast forward to the present day: She often has bad days and can't do all the things she would like to do because she ended up depending on her partner.

Limiting beliefs are another powerful anchor. We all have an inner critic, but when we give in to it, our lives become a nightmare. If you believe that you are not good enough, pretty enough, or smart enough, or if you think you don't deserve to be loved, most likely you will accept an abusive partner simply because you feel lucky that a man sees you as a "catch." You believe that, if you lose this guy, it will be a long time before you find a new one—if, in fact, you ever do.

Georgia was once married to the man of her dreams. They were both young, beautiful, passionate, and madly in love. As time went by, her husband became a stranger. They separated after a bitter divorce and over 15 years spent under the same roof. Georgia needed a few good months before she got back into the dating game. Freaks, womanizers, and drunkards knocked at her heart's door, making her believe all good men were taken. That's when Mark showed up—tall, stylish, experienced, and still attractive despite his grays. He took her to fancy dinners, helped her pick out new furniture for her bedroom, and let her vent without trying to fix the problem. When Georgia found out that Mark was married, it was too late. She was head over heels in love with him. Besides, a woman in her 40s couldn't be picky. Mark promised he would leave his wife, but he never did. Georgia got used to celebrating the holidays by herself, crying herself to sleep.

Building your identity on your relationship can also prevent you from making the right choice for you. In this scenario, the man's attention (I'm not using the word "love" because where there is toxicity, there is no love) validates you, makes you feel worthy and desired, and gives you a life purpose. Losing the relationships feels like losing your identity, as if a gust of wind would strip you naked on the street.

That's precisely how I felt when my boyfriend went to work abroad for six months. Although I had so much going on in my life (studying in college and working a job I loved as a radio host), the moment he said good-bye, I felt as if all the blood had left my body. I suddenly felt lost, like I belonged nowhere and to no one. All at once, life wasn't worth living and the world became a dangerous place. With envious eyes, I looked at other couples holding hands. I was myself only when he came back home once a month.

The more you accept a situation that doesn't honor you, the less self-esteem you have. No matter how your mind tries to justify acting against your own good, your soul knows the truth. You can never fool your soul. It knows that if only you'd follow its guidance, you'd find happiness and love without compromising.

The less self-esteem you have, the more bitter you become. You also feel that everybody else knows what's going on in your head. You act guarded and are less likely to go out and meet new people. No wonder your toxic partner has such a grip on you.

Michelle was seeing a guy for a few months when, the day before their first holiday, she told him a white lie to avoid an unpleasant conversation. It never crossed her mind that he had a surveillance camera in the living room and had seen her letting his Husky inside to shelter her from the scorching heat. He caused a terrible scene and told her that from then on, he could never trust her. However, they could still have sex if she wanted and go on the trip together.

They had sex that very night but, instead of his usual display of love and tenderness, he went to sleep in the guest bedroom. Michelle decided to ignore her intuition and stick to the initial plan. The holiday was a nightmare that continued after they got back. By then, she was convinced that no decent guy would date a woman like her.

Habit keeps people together, even when things go sour. You become so accustomed to a particular lifestyle, to what you know, to that man in your life, that you can't picture your life without him. If you let go of the relationship, you will free up a tremendous amount of energy and time you won't quite know how to use.

Habit's trusted partner is the comfort zone. Believe it or not, pain can be a comfort zone because it is familiar. You know when it comes, how it manifests, and what you must do to appease it. It is the same in a toxic relationship. The suffering becomes predictable and ingrained in your life like a tattoo.

However, you know how to deal with it. You know how to deal with this toxic partner of yours. You wouldn't know how to deal with the unknown. At this very moment, a man who truly loves you and wants the best for you is the unknown. He doesn't have to stay like that.

Habit kept me in a relationship for a couple of years. We didn't fight, probably because we didn't live together. We led almost separate lives. However, I knew my boyfriend well and also was free to do whatever I wanted whenever I wanted. The situation didn't help heal my limiting beliefs about relationships. For example, I envisioned that a committed relationship would be a tedious grind. That's precisely what I experienced. We never did anything fun or exciting. By having him in my life, I had drastically reduced my chances of meeting someone who would have been a proper match. Arielle Ford, one of the top international experts in relationships, explains that we must make room in our lives for the perfect partner—room in our closets, our driveways, and certainly in our beds.

All spiritual teachers agree that attachment leads to unhappiness. However, attachment keeps people together when nothing else does. Often, it is mistaken for love. The easiest way to know which one you are experiencing is to gauge your feelings. Love frees and inspires you. Attachment triggers insecurity, expectations, possessiveness, and selfishness. Attachment is about fulfilling your needs and inner void. Losing someone you're attached to is painful because you take it personally. When you love someone, you're happy for their happiness, even when you part ways.

You can also hope that, by humoring and pleasing your partner, you'll make him act the way he used to. However, you can't, at least not like that. A guy once told me, "We all put our best foot forward when we court a woman. It doesn't necessarily mean we'll keep at it once we get her attention."

Addiction is a stronger form of attachment. Some people are addicted to being a victim because the situations in which they play this role validate their egos and their beliefs about life. A woman may be sexually addicted to her toxic partner. She may find the emotional rollercoaster he puts her through to be the only excitement in her dull and boring life. Addiction creates the illusion that you can't live without that person.

Ultimately, everything boils down to a lack of trust in the flow of life and in the notion that everything can work out for the best. When you don't trust life, you try to control things and let the mind take the driver's seat. Inevitably, the mind will take you down the same beaten path. You must take a different road to observe new scenery or have another vantage point from which to view the old one.

Taking a different road requires you to distance yourself from your partner and to let go of the past. Leaving a toxic relationship isn't enough if your thoughts and feelings stay behind. When you harbor regrets, resentments, anger, and frustration, true love eludes you.

If you want a healthy and happy couple relationship, you must first become a happy and emotionally healthy woman. This may sound daunting or totally unfair, but look at the silver lining.

What if you can experience love in your life simply by taking care of yourself? When you change your inner landscape, your outer landscape changes. We always attract people and circumstances that vibrate on the same frequency as our own. You have the power to create a miraculous life and attract a loving man who will cherish and adore you.

You just need to take the first step and become aware of what's going on in your life right now.

Anchor Checklist:

What makes you stay in a toxic relationship? Look at the list below and check the items that fit your situation. Then have an honest conversation and see if they are real.

The next step is to imagine yourself in the situation(s) you fear (let's say being single or being the talk of the town) and find the benefit.

O Fear of being single	O Feelings of love
O Fear of being attacked	O Pity
O Fear of what other people will say	O Lack of self-confidence
O Financial challenges	O Lack of self-worth
O Addiction	O Kids
O Habit	O Beliefs
O Fear of the unknown	

Step 1:
Dust Off the Magnifying Glass

One late afternoon in November, I had to drive to North LA for an open mic event. I decided to meet a friend at Griffith Observatory beforehand and go from there. At 5 p.m., a thick blanket of darkness had already embraced the city and a pedestrian could outrun even the fastest car.

I remember the situation as if it had happened minutes ago. Google Maps put me on a string of narrow, winding roads until I ended up in Laurel Canyon. For those of you who don't know, Laurel Canyon looks gorgeous at daytime but, because of the poor street lighting, can be pretty daunting at night. Cell phones don't really work in this neighborhood—at least mine wasn't. A mile or more into it, I had no service and no Google

Maps access. I pressed forward at a slower speed until there were scarcely any homes on the slopes. I was the only driver on the road.

Finally, I had to accept what my intuition had been telling me: I was lost. It was only then that I pulled over, put myself together, and came up with a plan.

In life, we can't change a situation or fix something that isn't working for us until we become aware of the problem and decide to "pull over." Our gut may tell us that we are treading on a different path than the one meant for us or that a person is behaving dishonestly, yet we ignore it. That's because, if we followed our gut, we would have to leave our comfort zones and step into the unknown or maybe admit we'd made a bad choice.

Ironically, by trying to keep us safe, our ego keeps us trapped and causes us to miss crucial growing opportunities. When we live too much in our heads and too little in our hearts, and when those two don't work together, the mind always wins.

When you see a happy couple, the feeble voice of your heart might make itself heard, telling you that your relationship doesn't honor you. But your mind will tell you that nobody's perfect; you're not worthy of love; you've put so much time and energy into your relationship; you can't afford to leave. The list could go on forever.

Know that the Universe always supports the brave ones who follow their destinies. It's never too late to love and accept yourself for who you are and to experience a fulfilling couple relationship with a partner who loves, cherishes, and treats you like his queen.

However, your mind has to get it. And it won't get it until your mind becomes aware that the potential damage and danger of staying in a toxic relationship exceeds the damage that could result from ending it.

Let me ask you a question. What do you do when you want to check your complexion? You know ... see what it really looks like, decide whether it's time for a day at a beauty parlor. You don't glance into the bathroom mirror from a distance. You use a magnifying glass.

When was the last time you looked at your relationship? It's time to dust off the magnifying glass and do it now.

Lists are among the best tools you can use to work around the blind spots of your mind.

Set aside time for yourself, at least an hour. I recommend choosing a place other than home (if you live together) or work. It must be a place where you feel safe to have peace of mind. A park can work. The beach, too, if you live nearby, or even a public library.

Put pen to paper. Don't use an app on your phone or computer. Writing in longhand fosters calm and positive thinking. According to scientists, handwriting also increases neural activity in specific sections of the brain, similar to meditation, and sharpens the mind. This is exactly what you need to correctly take this step in your new life.

Divide the piece of paper into two columns and get ready to make your first list.

In the left column, write down what is it about your partner that causes you discomfort (cons). In the right column, write down what is it about him that makes you happy (pros).

Don't think too hard about it. Just let the information come to you.

If your relationship is utterly toxic, you'll probably have to extend the cons column to the back of the page and have little to note in the pros section. If so, don't force yourself to come up with stuff and embellish things. Just accept the situation the way it is. The goal of this step is for you to get a clear picture of where you are, to see things that you might have ignored, to become aware of your emotions.

On your list, put big things and little things.

In the pros column, you could include sexual chemistry, good looks, intelligence, and the fact that he makes you breakfast. In the cons column, you could include demanding, overbearing, jealous, stingy, unreliable, unfaithful, demeaning, and so on. You know your partner the best.

See how the items on this list compare to those on your "ideal partner" list. I'm sure that "cheating," "deceit," or "emotional manipulator" don't appear in the qualities section. To the contrary, they might have a well-deserved place in the deal-breaker column.

As you can see, the list about your current partner will help you see him for who he really is and to determine the extent to which he meets your requirements. This list will also help you further down the road to healing and happiness. Make sure you keep it because you will need it.

The second list will help you assess your overall state of wellbeing in the relationship. You can name it "Relationship Pros and Cons."

People around us, especially our life partners and those with whom we spend most of our time, have a huge impact on us. Their energy, thoughts, behavior, feelings, and thoughts can alter the quality of our existence, whether or not we realize it. Of course, the more aware you become, the more you love and accept yourself and the less other people influence you. But until then, you must be really careful about the company you keep.

Every human interaction entails an exchange of energy. This exchange increases between the partners of a couple relationship because sexual intercourse builds an etheric tube between their second chakras. This pipe allows energy to circulate back and forth between them and solidifies over time. Spiritual teachers say that it takes about seven years to go away after you stop being sexually involved with that person. Guess what happens when one of the partners harbors negative feelings, emotions, and thoughts? The other person gets some of them, too.

It is also said that once you enter a couple relationship or marriage with another person, you take their karma. Some men, for example, get incredibly successful once they become involved with a certain woman, only to lose everything if the man decides to break up with her, or if she dies.

All that being said, your couple relationship impacts all aspects of your life. Is it a positive or good one? "The Relationship Pros and Cons List" will help you figure that out more clearly, although deep down in your heart, you already know the truth.

Divide your list into different life sectors. What impact does this relationship have on every aspect of your life? Health, life dreams, career, hobbies, family, friends, finances? Again, write down the pros and cons for each of them.

Let's start with health—physical, emotional, mental. Do you feel more energized, pain-free, in better overall health now than when you were single? Do you feel inspired, uplifted, creative in the flow every day? Do you feel that you're safe, protected, appreciated, and loved and that you're living the best possible life?

Or do you feel drained, as though you're walking on shifting sands? Does your back hurt all the time and do you catch a cold quickly? Stressful environments, repressed emotions, and fear weaken our immune system and lower our vibration, making us more susceptible to ailments, diseases, and even accidents.

What about your career? How are things in this department? Do you know what you want? Are you giving it your best and do you feel that you're on an upward curve? Are you making steady progress towards your goals or, on the other hand, are things not working so well anymore? When your relationship consumes you, you start to occasionally slip because it's hard to focus on anything else.

How are your finances? Are you stable? Are you seeing an increase in wealth and prosperity? Or not? Finances imply more than your monthly paycheck or business revenue. They involve everything about money, including unexpected loss— something expensive breaking down in the house, car accidents, the loss of objects.

Next, look at your life goals and dreams. Maybe you dream of one day giving up your nine-to-five job to become a painter or a writer or to start your own business. To do this, you must take daily steps and maybe learn new skills. Where are you on this path? Did you forget about it because your partner takes up all your spare time or tells you that you're going to fail? Or are you almost there because of his support and encouragement?

Hobbies play an essential role in our wellbeing. They connect us with our inner child, keeping us playful and alive while leading us to our life purpose. They represent an agreeable opportunity to meet like-minded people and are a reflection of our true essence. So, do you make time to nurture your hobbies? Or do you need to look up the definition of "hobby" in the dictionary?

Last but not least, look at your relationships with your family and friends. Someone who is cut off from their dear ones falls prey more easily to a toxic partner. We all need to bond with other people. When no one else is around, we end up ignoring reality. We're like a rabbit that mistakes a gun for a carrot.

How often do you see your family members now as compared to before? Are you still on good terms, or have you stopped talking to them because your partner told you they can't stand him? Do you spend time with your friends, or do they avoid you because you never listen to their advice and always complain about your relationship?

Once you complete your list, you'll probably discover that something is "off" in each one of these areas—more "off" in some areas and less "off" in others. We are whole beings, which means that usually, when something isn't working in one area of our lives, the other areas suffer, too. That's because, at every moment, you vibrate at a specific frequency, which attracts a matching reality. The good news is that once you learn how to do it, it is easy to raise your vibration and keep it high.

But for now, feelings of resentment, anger, humiliation, frustration, and guilt may arise once you finish making the lists. You may feel used, abused, and taken advantage of. Allow yourself to feel that way (after all, you've repressed it for so long) without judging or being hard on yourself.

However, don't rush into starting a fight with him. Don't blame him or threaten him or pack up your things and risk returning at his first phone call.

For now, these lists are just for you. Nobody has to know you're going through this process (other maybe your closest and most trustworthy friend). At this stage, focus only on yourself, on getting to know how you feel and what's best for you, instead of making a dramatic change. Just like a bird that has been caged for a long time, you need time to gather strength and fly again.

Remember that everything happens for a reason. In particular, remember that you are not a victim. You are a powerful creator-being who can turn things around in the blink of an eye. You have the ability to dissolve the patterns that don't serve you anymore, especially if you follow your intuition. As your most trustworthy compass, intuition always points you in the right direction. It shows you the path to joy, abundance, fulfillment, health, and love. Each time you don't follow your intuition, you will pay the price.

A few years ago, I matched with a guy on Tinder. I used online dating apps for a while because I believe that love can walk in through any door, anytime. From the very beginning, the situation seemed too good to be true, or maybe my doubts about ever finding the right man kicked in. Michael's deep blue eyes mesmerized me. The mere touch of his hand as he helped me out of the car made my body tingle. We could talk for hours about everything and nothing as if we had known each other for a lifetime.

After we went on a couple of fun dates, he disappeared without saying a word. A few weeks later, he surfaced, saying he missed me and couldn't wait for us to get together again. He apologized for his behavior and confessed he had some unresolved "issues" that he had dealt with. Therefore, we could start our relationship with a clean slate.

I decided to give him another chance only to find myself going through the same scenario again and again. He would vanish into thin air for a while, then come back with a box full of chocolates and a mouth full of excuses.

When we take the time to have a thorough look at our relationships, when we are honest with ourselves and see the truth, we will perceive the patterns. Patterns are recurring situations that are woven into our lives, often with different people. Each relationship teaches us something, helps us grow and evolve. However, when we miss this opportunity, the lesson stays and repeats itself with various partners. Early in my Reiki initiation days, I asked my master what to do about the man I was seeing at the time. She told me that I had two options: "Stay and learn what you need to learn with this guy, or leave him and learn it with the next one."

When you identify the recurring pattern in your relationship, you can see your couple dynamics more clearly. You will also know what to expect and how to grasp your partner's motivations and personality. You finally realize that, no matter what you do or how hard you try, you always end up in the same place.

You do your best to look attractive all the time, and people around you acknowledge it, yet he criticizes you. He promises to do different things for you but always has a good excuse to not follow through. You strive to meet his needs, yet he still finds something to complain about. He tells you that you're the love of his life, but he keeps you at arm's length. Your time together always ends in an argument. There's nothing wrong with disagreeing and having a different opinion about things, but constant struggling and fighting indicate an unhealthy relationship. Sometimes, walking away is the only solution to breaking a toxic pattern.

That's what I did a year into my dysfunctional relationship with Michael. Eventually, I found the strength to let go of him and put a stop to my misery. It became effortless once I realized what I truly wanted out of a relationship and my life partner.

Pattern Checklist

Toxic recurring behavior:

1._____

2._____

3._____

4._____

5._____

Toxic recurring words:

1._____

2._____

3._____

4._____

5._____

Step 2:
Listen to the Whispers of Your Soul

My friend, Marianne, had no idea she would fall in love when she boarded the plane back home from Brussels. From the corner of her eye, she had glimpsed a tall, dark-haired, handsome man waiting in line a few feet away from her. She told herself a guy like that would never see her.

Not only did he see her, but he also engaged her in a conversation that lasted the whole flight. When they landed, he begged for her phone number. At first, Marianne was tempted to say no and let fate decide their future. After all, it had assigned them adjoining seats. But the look in his eyes—a mix of admiration and genuine interest—made her give in.

That evening, before she went to bed, Marianne took off her clothes and, for the very first time in a long time, had a good look at herself in the full-length mirror. She had detected something else shining in the man's eyes besides admiration and interest. She had seen desire. That didn't come across as a surprise. Marianne had had enough experience with men to know that the right attitude can be sexier than long legs and the perfect body.

However, she wondered, would he still want her when he saw her soft white skin, big stress belly, and huge thighs? The cellulite on her butt, the sagging bags under her triceps? What if another woman caught his attention on his way home?

The young man, a graphic designer for an advertising agency and the bass player in a renowned rock band, called her that very evening. A few days later, he came over for dinner. Marianne's five-star cooking, along with her infamous laughter and bubbly personality, always attracted other people's praise. Dinner led to a midnight conversation on the living-room sofa and then wild sex on the floor.

Her soft white skin, flabby arms, and huge thighs simply turned him into a sex-machine.

After that night, Marianne felt she had finally found the man of her dreams. They had not only amazing chemistry but also the best conversations ever. Her lover was interested in philosophy and current affairs. He devoured books and was incredibly smart.

As time went by, the relationship blossomed ... or so she thought. Busy with work, they exchanged messages on Facebook during the week and then met at her place during the weekend. At first, Marianne didn't mind not doing what normal couples usually do—go out together, spend time with mutual friends. After all, the sex was so amazing. But then all kinds of thoughts started bugging her. After a few months of hot weekends, she finally suggested that they go to the movies together. It was only then that her "match made in heaven" admitted that, although he desired her sexually, he would be embarrassed to be seen in public with a woman like her.

"Please don' t take it personally," he said. "It's got nothing to do with you. In fact, you're the only woman who makes me feel safe and complete. The only woman I want to spend time with. But I have a public image to defend."

Marianne swallowed her tears and chose to hear only the words she wanted to hear. She told herself that good sex was hard to find those days and accepted his terms and conditions.

As time went by, her smile faded and she laughed less. Her job suddenly drained her. Her family kept mistreating her. She told herself that all the good men her age were taken.

I asked her to describe one of those "good men." She needed a few minutes to think about it, then came up with "successful, good-looking, and stable." The list she had made in her early 20s included more attributes, but she couldn't remember it. Anyway, it wouldn't have served her because she had come to terms with her current situation. She was also used to living alone, so a full-blown relationship in which the two partners end up living together wouldn't have worked.

Marianne's dark eyes contradicted the self-imposed smile on her face. I could tell that she yearned for more than just weekly great sex. She was looking for excuses to stay in a toxic relationship.

I shared with her the story of another friend of mine, Michelle.

Michelle had a bitter and toxic marriage that ended in disaster. A highly successful life coach and author, she decided to use this experience to embrace her femininity and learn more about herself. Instead of shutting off her heart or rushing into a new relationship, she healed, learned, and found out what she really wanted from a life partner and a couple relationship.

Michelle made a list of about 20 must-have qualities in a man. Then she made a list of the deal-breakers. Shortly after, at an event, she met her One: the man who became her second husband. They have been happily married for a few good years now, built a successful life-coaching business together, and had a wonderful son.

The law of attraction works in every aspect of your life. You draw into your life what you vibrate. When you don't know what you want and when you doubt life, you attract the kind of people and situations that vibrate at this frequency. The only way to turn things around is to change your vibration.

How can you increase your vibration? Love, compassion, appreciation, and joy are all high-frequency vibratory states. We'll get more into that later in this book.

For now, I would like you to focus on the type of experiences you want in your relationship. How would you like to feel?

Women, especially young women, focus a lot on what their man should be and look like and less on how they would like to feel in a relationship. Also, they tend to create their lists of the attributes of an ideal man based on the models imposed by society, family, or friends, and less on what they want and need.

When I was a teenager and very young woman, intelligence, talent, and looks drew me. I had a soft spot for dark-haired, brown-eyed, tall, athletic guys. Even better if they played guitar in a rock band. Things shifted once I hit my mid-30s. I began to care less about looks and more about the experience that the guy provided. I even ended up falling in love with a man because of the way he treated me and made me feel.

How would you like your partner to treat you? How would you like to feel? By answering these two questions and comparing your output with your current situation, you will get a clearer picture of where you are now. Your mind will be able to internalize the situation and, maybe, realize that it's more dangerous to stay or continue along the same path than to make a change or leave.

If you want to be treated like a queen or princess, don't be ashamed to admit it. Put it down on paper. There's nothing wrong with it. Although it's cool to be a feminist, it's cool to not be one, too. Allow yourself to be a woman and to be treated as such. It is such a blessing, and it makes the man happy.

You may argue that making such a list would take romance out of the equation. Rest assured, it won't. But it certainly saves you time, suffering, and tears.

You don't have to walk around with a piece of paper and a pen hidden in your purse and pretend you need to use the restroom so you can check some of the boxes. You will still go through the process of meeting someone, feeling connection or attraction, and getting to know that person. Your soul will sing a happy song when you meet someone who matches its calling, and the sparkles of romance will fly higher than ever.

Besides, how can you choose the right person if you don't know what you want and what makes you happy?

I highly appreciate chivalrous behavior in a man; it makes me feel seen, appreciated, and respected. I enjoy it when he gets the door for me, carries the grocery bags, or walks on the right side of the curb. I also appreciate a man who makes me feel safe and protected, who uplifts me and inspires me to be the best version of myself. I love communicating freely about anything, anytime, but also being in the same room together and not necessarily talking—just doing our own thing. I also love creating stuff (from books to businesses) so I want a partner with whom I can create something. As a Taurus woman, I find that sensuality plays a vital role in my life; therefore, I must have a healthy and fulfilling sex life.

Pretty high on my desired experiences list is "feeling comfortable being myself/authentic." I need a partner who accepts and loves me, warts and all, and who doesn't make me walk on eggshells.

These are just a few of the things on my list. I hope they will inspire you to create your own. Make sure you add all the experiences you desire and that are essential to you. You, not your friends, family, society, and other people. Remember, nothing is too odd, too much, or too strange.

One thing, though, should be at the top of your list: feeling safe.

You need to feel safe physically, emotionally, and mentally so you can blossom, open up, grow, and be yourself.

You feel safe when you can express your emotions, thoughts, and opinions, what you want and what you don't want, without being punished, threatened, or belittled.

You feel safe when you follow your dreams and passions without fearing your partner will try to make you feel guilty about it.

You feel safe when you spend time with your family and friends, and sometimes in solitude, knowing your partner won't have a jealousy spell.

You feel safe when you can say "no" because you know your partner would never physically abuse you.

You feel safe when you can be vulnerable and express your fears and worries because your partner would never use them against you or to manipulate you.

You feel safe when your partner behaves in a way that shows he'll be there for you when the going gets tough, no matter what.

In 2011, Turia Pitt, one of Australia's most inspirational and courageous women, suffered burns to 65 percent of her body. She also lost her fingers and a thumb. The ravaging effects are still visible; however, her boyfriend, Michael Hoskin, stayed by her side. He gave up his job as a police officer to take care of her, and after she got out of the hospital, he proposed to her. In a magazine interview, he declared that she is such a beautiful and amazing person and that he loves her soul.

You need someone in your life who can see you beyond your physical body, who can "see" your soul. And you need to listen to the whispers of your soul to finally know what's best for you.

This may be new to you, but why not give it a try? After all, your old methods have led you to where you are today, reading this book.

If you've been prodding your mind for answers to questions such as "What do I want to experience in a relationship?" and "How do I want to feel in a relationship?", ask the same questions of your soul. But don't rush it. You need time to quiet your mind, slow down the beating of your heart, and tune in to the energy within you.

It's like sailing on open water to see the dolphins. You won't do it on a gloomy, windy day when the mighty ocean throws angry waves at you. You'd rather have the experience on a sunny and peaceful day when you can see the shiny black backs of the dolphins under the tranquil surface.

The soul may give you the same answers as the mind, but most likely, many of them will differ. It will also offer you a very precious gift: stability and balance.

Your soul harbors an infinite supply of power and wisdom. By connecting with it, you connect with the almighty power of the Universe. You gather strength. You feel less afraid. You realize that, somehow, somebody is watching you all the time, ready to take your hand and pull you out of the lowest pit.

The Universe is governed by a highly benevolent and loving force, one that is continuously watching over us and that always has our back. Call it the Source, the Infinite Spirit, God. The essence is the same.

You must connect with this power now more than ever. It's probably the only true ally you have on your journey out of your toxic relationship.

This parable speaks volume.

A man on his deathbed had a conversation with God. As we went back in time, his life looked like a stroll on the beach. Through the good times, he noticed that two sets of footprints marked the sand, as if two people had walked side by side. Through the bad times, though, he could see only one set of footprints.

The man saddened. Many of his friends had deserted him when he had encountered hardships.

"You, too," he whispered. "You abandoned me when I needed you the most."

"No, I didn't. I just carried you when you couldn't stand on your feet," God replied.

This infinite power looks after you, too. You can access it anytime because it's in your soul. When you do, you step into your power and allow the people around you to step into theirs.

PLAYTIME

My Ideal Partner Checklist

Top 20 Qualities

1._____   11._____

2._____   12._____

3._____   13._____

4._____   14._____

5._____   15._____

6._____   16._____

7._____   17._____

8._____   18._____

9._____   19._____

10._____   20._____

How do I want to feel in a relationship?

_____

_____

_____

_____

_____

_____

_____

_____

_____

_____

_____

What types of experiences do I want to have in a relationship?

_____

_____

_____

_____

_____

_____

_____

_____

_____

_____

Step 3:
Unplug the Negativity Cord

From day to day, things were getting worse. I could barely recognize the man I had fallen in love with months earlier and I hardly recognized myself. The joy-filled, uplifting, energetic, assertive me was hiding somewhere out of reach. The other me—fearful, meek, feisty—stirred the boat right into heated arguments and awkward moments of silence. And if this didn't already put enough weight on my shoulders, my whole life seemed to be heading in the wrong direction. Nothing made sense anymore.

Almost at my wits' end, I started looking for support. You see, it's perfectly okay to reach out for help. Even the bravest, wisest, and most knowledgeable of us sometimes need guidance or a shoulder to lean on. That's how I found out that once we're caught in a spiral of negativity, it's impossible to swing back into positivity. The spiral of negativity acts very much like a strong current running under the surface of a rapid river. Once it catches you, it pulls you away from the shore and drags you to the bottom unless you find a raft or a log to cling to.

In the case of a life filled with negativity, you must reach a neutral point before you can restore love and positivity.

When you have a toxic relationship, you are like a fish in a tank. However, instead of water, you swim in negativity. That's because toxic relationships generate anxiety, stress, fear, and pressure, to name just a few of the fallouts. And when these emotions control your life, your ability to make the right decisions, see things clearly, and act according to your best interest decreases.

You need to break the cycle of negativity right now. You need fresh water; you need fresh air.

You need to surround yourself with the right people.

If your own critical voice, and that of your partner, are the only ones you hear every day, it's time for you to listen to other voices. You may live in a beautiful apartment in a great neighborhood, but if you're in a toxic relationship, it probably feels like a prison. Just like a prisoner, you dream about the days when the sun's rays caressed your face and when joy and laughter filled your life. However, unlike a prisoner, you are free to step outside any time you want.

One of the best ways to unplug the negativity cord is to spend more time with people other than your partner. This includes family and friends —people whom you may have pushed away, whether intentionally or not. People who've been through a similar situation and who can understand you. People who share your passions and core values. People who want to serve other people.

No matter who they are or how you find them, look for people who are positive and who lead fulfilling, joyful lives. Their energy is contagious and you are in a space where you must fill your own cup before you support or nurture others.

Look for people who see the best in you; who remind you about how great and amazing you are; who can help you rebuild your self-confidence, self-esteem, and self-worth.

Wallowing in your misery in front of other people is a waste of time. Instead of breaking free from your self-imposed prison, you add time to your sentence and turn a deaf ear to any words that might help you. People may want to help you, but they will get tired and walk away if you keep acting as though the Earth spins around your broken relationship. Therefore, when you meet, refrain from complaining. Instead, focus on topics other than how awful your partner is. Once you regain your inner strength and balance, you will be able to effortlessly make the best decision about your relationship.

My friend Angela is one of the smartest, most beautiful women I know. Yet, she always ends up with the wrong man. The scenario is pretty much always the same. Fireworks of joy at the beginning, followed by bitterness and sorrow. Every time we get together, I enumerate her many qualities that could make any man fall at her feet. But she's so focused on her problem that my words never get through. The negativity tide in her life is so strong, she can't fight it.

So, wisely use your relationships with the people who care about and support you. You don't know how long they're going to be around. Life works in mysterious ways, and you never know when an unexpected event will take away someone you cherish.

Maximize the time you spend together to divert your attention away from your relationship. Have fun and meaningful conversations; do things you love; visit nice places that you all enjoy; discover new restaurants or cafés; discuss books and movies; be of service to others; tell jokes and laugh. Choose one or two friends with whom you can discuss your projects and dreams. Ask them to tell you what they appreciate and love about you. Then, write those things on a piece of paper. At first, the items on your list may sound like somebody else's. However, carry that piece of paper in your wallet and look at it every day until you remember who you truly are and recognize yourself in that list.

Every week, carve out time for the positive. special people in your life. Meet up with them, even if only for an hour, after work, or during your lunch break.

Soon, you will realize that there's life beyond your relationship and that your partner isn't the only person on the planet other than you.

Being single doesn't necessarily equal loneliness, sadness, or boredom. Every day can be full of meaning and joy, whether or not you are in a relationship, provided you allow it to be so. The decision is yours.

My next favorite tool is mindfulness.

In southwest San Bernardino County, in Southern California, lies BAPS Shri Swaminarayan, the first earthquake-proof Mandir in the world. Constructed from 35,000 pieces of meticulously hand-carved Italian Carrara marble and Pink Indian sandstone, this Hindu temple puts the mind on pause mode with its breathtaking beauty. Inside, it's impossible to not stay in the present moment. The intricate carvings depict a mosaic of tales of inspiration, devotion, and dedication, along with historical figures from Hinduism. For a moment, they make the visitor forget about any problems and challenges in life. The visitor is inspired to sense the magic and infinite power of the Universe that glues everything together, to tap into it and be inspired to up his game.

I get the same feeling when I hike into a forest in Sequoia National Park, look at the waterfalls gushing over the edges of the high stern cliffs in Yosemite Park, watch the sunset on the beach, or admire a painting, as well as when music touches my heart at a concert.

You may ask: What does that have to do with unplugging from the negativity of a toxic relationship?

A lot! Earlier in the book, I mentioned that the first step toward solving your problem is to acknowledge it. The next step is to put yourself in a state of being—emotional, mental, and physical—which supports your efforts to make and act on the right decision.

When you spend time in nature, lose yourself in a song, or live in the now, you raise your vibration and step out of your ordinary mindset, which is governed by fear and limitations. Inadvertently, you practice mindfulness.

Mindfulness surpasses Instagram fads and life-style magazine "trending" columns. Mindfulness is a way of life that we don't learn in school. Instead, we stumble upon it accidentally when we immerse ourselves in something we love. It's a practice we take up consciously when we start tuning into our heart's calling.

When you practice mindfulness, you maintain a moment-by-moment awareness of your thoughts, your feelings, your body, and the surrounding environment. You stop reliving the past or worrying about the future.

You elevate a notch higher above the plane where your problem has been created. That is such a huge step ahead. As Albert Einstein put it, no problem can be solved from the same level of consciousness that created it.

Mindfulness will help you unplug from negativity by bringing balance into your life and restoring your connection to the Source energy. This connection plays a crucial role in your life. It is as if you have a spare battery that always fuels your energy tanks and that makes you feel whole. It also gives you the guidance that no friend, family member, or therapist can provide.

When we are connected to the Source energy, we literally become different people and our lives change. Our eating habits change (we eat less and healthier), our sleep pattern changes, our perspective on life changes. We realize that we're perfect and complete just the way we are and that we don't need a life partner to be happy. Mindfulness also restores self-love and self-appreciation.

One of the main reasons people stay in toxic relationships is the veiled fear that life would be so much worse without the other person in it. Mindfulness can dispel this illusion. You just have to start using the right techniques.

*

*   *

Meditation is one of the most common and best-known mindfulness techniques. Meditation puts your brain on a different frequency (Alpha) than the one on which you usually operate (Beta). When you're in Alpha, the conscious mind comes to a standstill. You can access a deeper level of consciousness and fire up new neuronal paths.

You can meditate in various ways. You can sit on the floor in the Lotus position or in a chair, your spine upright, your feet and arms uncrossed. You can listen to meditation music or guided meditations, or you can sit in silence. If you're just starting, make sure to pick a quiet place where nobody will disturb you. As you progress along your path, you will be able to meditate anywhere, even at a loud construction site.

*

*   *

Affirmations go hand in hand with meditation.
Neuroplasticity works best when the brain operates on lower

frequencies such as 8Hz-14Hz (Alpha) or even 4Hz-8Hz (Delta). Affirmations work because the more often we hear a message, the more likely we are to believe it. Affirmations are powerful tools for counteracting negative messages.

You can use ready-made affirmations (I recommend Louise Hay and Florence Scovel Shinn's books) or create your own. The affirmations must be written in the present tense and focus on your desired outcome/goals.

In the case of someone suffering from the pressure of a toxic relationship, positive affirmations can work miracles in restoring self-confidence, self-worth, self-love, and self-acceptance.

Here are some affirmations that worked for me:

I love and accept myself just as I am.

I am happy. I am healthy. I am worthy. I am mighty.

I now deserve, accept, and attract the best of what life has to offer.

I am a miraculous being leading a miraculous life.

Spending time in nature ranks high among favorite mindfulness techniques. Turn off your phone, get out of the city and the crowds of people, and explore nature. Look for pristine places. Listen to the chirping of the birds and the rustle of the leaves. Fill your lungs with fresh air and your eyes with the vivid colors around you. Take it all in with each breath.

When you connect with nature, you attune yourself to the energy of Mother Earth, who nourishes us every moment. You expand beyond your thoughts, problems, and worries.

Take advantage of this time of the day to breathe consciously— another powerful mindfulness technique. When we were babies, we took full, deep breaths, conducting the air into our lungs and bellies. Later in life, we forgot how to do this. The more we operate from a "fight or flight" mode, the shallower our breathing gets.

Breath is life force energy. The more air we inhale, the stronger we are and the better our brain works. A deep, steady breath will always decrease our stress level because it sends a signal to the body that we are safe and that everything is okay.

Everything feels okay when our thoughts, words, and actions are in harmony. This usually happens when we immerse ourselves into something we absolutely love.

I firmly believe that every single action that fosters inner harmony and helps us stay in the present moment is a powerful mindfulness tool.

Mindfulness can be practiced anywhere, anytime, by anyone. You don't have to sit in a church pew, wear white, draw mandalas, join your fingertips into Hindu mudras, or chant Sanskrit mantras. Of course, they can help, but when the mind keeps fidgeting or racing, these techniques lose their effectiveness.

One of my dear friends loves to clean her home during the weekend. It keeps her focused on the now and allows her to take a break from her monkey mind. Cleaning is her mindfulness tool. Another friend loves mountain biking at high altitudes. Some people get in the zone by dancing, painting, writing, or even cooking.

The more you stay in the zone, the easier it is to use another powerful mindfulness tool, which is gratitude. Although it may sound counterintuitive, gratitude has the power to remove the negativity—at least some if not all—from a toxic relationship.

*

*   *

If you've been in a toxic relationship for a while now, most likely you have a long list of things that cause you stress and pain. When these are not addressed and expressed healthily, they calcify into a wall of resentment and generate an underground current of tension.

Not voicing your frustration doesn't mean you don't feel it. It doesn't mean that you don't hold your partner responsible for all that's going sideways in your life.

It simply means that, for one reason or another, you decide to keep it inside or occasionally vent it to your best friends. Although this can help you release some tension, it's not the most effective long-term solution.

Janice was seeing Rob for about a year, but his shortcomings were all she talked about. Every week, she had a new story about Rob failing her again. He forgot their anniversary, was late for dinner, promised to spend the night at her place and then canceled without a solid reason, failed to notice her new hair color. She hated the way he kept her on her toes. She felt unseen and disrespected.

We told her to break up with him if he made her unhappy. Janice said she loved him. They had a great time together and he was the funniest, most brilliant guy she knew. Then she would start complaining about his attitude again.

Eventually, Janice decided to embark on her journey of love, which helped her realize the deeper cause of her frustration and resentment. It had little to do with Rob's actions and more to do with the emotions they triggered. Janice felt unworthy, unseen, taken for granted, not woman enough, disrespected.

She realized that, if she wanted to make faster progress on her journey of love, she had to forgive Rob for a behavior she had condoned.

Most people have a hard time forgiving because they fear that forgiveness equals overlooking or weakness. Yet, as Mahatma Gandhi said, "Forgiveness is the attribute of the strong." People also need to see justice in action, and not giving vindication is part of it.

However, forgiveness is a gift you give to yourself. It has little to do with the other person. Forgiveness is a synonym for freedom from the shackles that bind you to the other person and to negativity.

Remember that the purpose of this chapter is to help you clear negativity from your life and restore your emotional, mental, and physical wellbeing.

Forgiveness plays a significant role in this process. As Marianne Williamson beautifully puts it, "There is no peace without forgiveness."

Imagine you're hiking a beautiful trail in a national park. The silence is so deep that you could hear the eagles' wings whooshing above your head—if only the whistles and horns attached to your shoes didn't make so much noise.

You'd love to climb up to the top and see the breathtaking view, but the backpack you're carrying is so heavy, you can barely move. You reach inside for a protein bar, but you find a brick. And another one. There's no food or water inside, nothing that you really need on your journey.

All this unnecessary weight symbolizes pent-up anger, resentment, hard feelings, and negativity. When you forgive, you detach yourself from the bells and whistles attached to your shoes. You empty your backpack of unnecessary bricks. You are finally free to enjoy life and reach the summit—to express your highest potential and live your life's purpose.

To forgive your partner, you don't have to wait to break up with him or wait for him to change. You can do it today and give yourself the necessary time. See, forgiveness isn't a decision you make. It's not a work of the mind or something you can force upon yourself. Forgiveness happens in the hidden folds of the heart. Your lips may utter, "I forgive you," but your heart may lag behind your intention.

In one of her "SuperSoul Podcast" episodes, Oprah Winfrey confessed that Maya Angelou gave her one of her favorite life-changing lessons, which has helped her stay away from toxic relationships. "When people tell you who they are, believe them," said the acclaimed writer. "They know themselves much better than you do. Now why are you angry?"

From the very beginning, a man always tells you what he's like, whether he uses words, behavior, or body language. The red flags and warning signs always show up in plain sight. However, you decide to ignore them. He's cute and has potential, so you want to continue the relationship. In the long term, these two qualities won't make you happy. So, why be angry with him?

You don't even have to tell him that you forgive him. He might not understand what you're forgiving him for. What you can do is sit in meditation and visualize putting down all the negativity that you've built around your partner and your relationship. Visualize how joy, harmony, and peace are replacing the negative emotions formerly stored in your body.

You can also write a letter to your partner. Express your feelings and use forgiveness to release both of you from a relationship that doesn't honor and serve you. You can burn the letter later.

The forgiveness process is complete once you feel peace when you think about, talk to, or interact with your partner and genuinely wish him all the best.

Because you have tried your hand at forgiveness, now is an excellent time to find out who else you need to forget. Then repeat the process. Start with yourself. I remember how hard I was on myself each time I rolled down the toxic relationship hill. My inner critic berated me for my inability to pull the plug on a situation that was wearing me out.

You may not realize it, but when you forgive yourself and other people, you reclaim your power, cast off the victim costume, and become the master of your life.

*

*   *

People who wear the victim costume attract to their lives people who are either rescuers or persecutors. In the case of a toxic relationship, it's most likely that the partner is critical, blaming, controlling, or acting superior.

We may be very successful in our jobs or have high status, but we constantly blame other people or life for every single minor misfortune. We put on the victim costume. Every time we feel, believe, or act as if someone is doing something (wrong) to us and react, we give our power to that person. When we feel jagged or angry, we lose the ability to make the right decisions. People with a keen sense of observation can deliberately push our buttons to control and manipulate us.

People who play the victim role feel too powerless to even consider changing their life situations. They think that others mean their harm. They keep talking about their sad stories and they put themselves down. They are cynical and pessimistic and they usually refuse to analyze their beliefs or improve their lives.

Sometimes, the roles can be reversed. The toxic partner—the one who always takes it on the loved one for how they feel—can be the victim, while the other partner is the rescuer. This type of personality is attracted to needy, damaged, or helpless people.

The rescuer usually provides support even when he doesn't want to. He also feels guilty when he doesn't rescue but expects to fail in his mission. Rescuing makes him feel more capable. The rescuer makes excuses for his partner and is hungry for constant reassurance in relationships.

Remember that if your partner is capable of rescuing himself, you take away his power to choose. Besides, you can't save someone who doesn't want to be rescued, no matter how far backwards you bend over.

Whether you play the victim or the rescuer, it is never too late to give up this role. It's not who you are at all. Why live your life on a small stage when a whole universe is at your feet?

The first step is to remember who you are. You are not your costume. You are not just your body. You are a unique human being, blessed with gifts and talents, who deserves to experience the best life can offer. You came here with a specific purpose: to enjoy life instead of crying yourself to sleep every night.

The second step is to remove the blame from your current life situation. You can do that when you see every person who challenges you and pushes your buttons as a teacher or mirror. According to the oriental philosophy, the souls make contracts between each other before incarnating into their human bodies. Some souls take on the role of aggressor or abuser to help other souls experience love and compassion, healing and progress. They stick to their end of the deal ... and so can you.

When you remove blame, you stop taking things personally. Instead of pitying yourself for what others did to you, you look at the situation and see the lesson. You start asking yourself questions such as:

Do I really love myself?

Where do I lie to myself?

Where don't I show up for myself?

Where do I fail myself?

Where am I being and acting cheap?

Why am I afraid to commit to somebody or a project?

I remember being in a relationship with a guy who lied every time he breathed. It was mostly small stuff, but it was still annoying to me at that time. The whole situation baffled me, especially because, overall, I considered myself an honest person. If that guy was a mirror, he reflected back to me a distorted view of myself. I reached out to my Reiki teacher for clarification.

"Maybe you're lying to yourself," she said. She was right. I was lying to myself by pretending I enjoyed being in that relationship when I didn't. A lie, even small and "white," is still a lie. Telling my mom I had eaten the pot of soup she had made for me when I had thrown away half of it counted as a lie. It would have served both of us more to tell her, in a gentle but straightforward way, that I wasn't a little girl and she didn't have to cook for me anymore.

Sometimes, the lesson of not taking things personally simply allows other people to be who they are without judgment or hard feelings.

The third empowering step you can take is to set healthy boundaries. Compassion, acceptance, and tolerance don't imply that other people, including your life partner, can walk all over you.

Although it sounds romantic to act like an open book and allow the other partner to pierce deep into your soul, you are entitled to your secret garden, particularly when you don't feel safe. It's okay to have this inner space where you plant the seeds of your dreams—seeds that only you can water.

This may sound counterintuitive, but you are entitled to privacy, even when you are in a relationship. Your partner doesn't have to know the passwords to your social media and email accounts. He has no right to search your phone or check your phone bill for incoming and outgoing calls.

Setting healthy boundaries means carving out time for yourself, your friends and family, your passions, and life goals. There is nothing wrong with spending time by yourself. You need "alone time" so that you always remember who you are and don't lose yourself.

It's perfectly fine to go out for lunch or dinner with your girlfriends. All the relationships in your life need nurturing, not just the couple one.

It's healthy, for you and the relationship, to take the dancing or painting classes you're dying to go attend, or to train for a marathon even when your partner isn't into it.

The more you step into your authentic self, follow your dreams, and stay true to yourself, the stronger you get. Your self-love, self-appreciation, and self-esteem grow exponentially. When you get to this point, nobody can tell you how to live your life.

By not allowing other people to manipulate you or treat you like a puppet on a string, you honor yourself and your partner.

Once you've learned the lesson and healed the trauma, you free him of the role of aggressor.

It's the same as when the curtain goes down at the end of the play and the actors leave the stage to take off their costumes. However, some of them can keep acting although the spectators have left the building.

As long as you get off stage and remove your costume, what the other actors do is no concern of yours. A whole life—unscripted and unpredictable, yet miraculous and mind-blowing—awaits you.

PLAYTIME

Mindfulness Tools at Work

Chose your favorite mindfulness tools and routines. You can use the list below as it is or you can create your own. Practice mindfulness every day. Write down the results. Here are mine.

MONDAY

Meditation
Result:_____

_____

_____

TUESDAY

Walk in the park
Result:_____

_____

_____

WEDNESDAY

Conscious breathing
Result:_____

_____

_____

THURSDAY

Forgiveness
Result:_____

_____

_____

FRIDAY

Gratitude
Result:_____

_____

_____

SATURDAY

Live in the now (for at least 5 minutes)
Result:_____

_____

_____

SUNDAY

Meditation:
Result:_____

_____

_____

Step 4:
Bring Your Superpowers Back to Life

I'm not big on rollercoasters, whether towering iron-made ones or gut-wrenching emotional ones. Those in amusement parks upset my stomach while those in my relationships have made me question my very existence. Whenever a past toxic relationship hit rock bottom and the illusion of love disappeared, I'd forget all about my dreams and aspirations and feel that a grain of sand mattered more.

Have you ever experienced this or something similar?

If you have, it shows that you need to build a new relationship with yourself—a relationship based on love, self-acceptance, self-confidence, compassion, and respect. Find out what makes your heart sing and abide by it. When you do, and when you act upon it, nobody can steal joy from you. The relationship you have with yourself lasts a lifetime and sets the foundation for all your other relationships. The more authentic you are, the better the relationship with yourself becomes.

As Miss Blanchard tells Addie Mare in one of my favorite novels, "Trusting the Currents" by Lynnda Pollyo, "don't ever let a boy change who you are."

To remember who you really are and build a solid relationship with yourself, you must get away from your toxic relationship. Start with as little as half an hour a day until you find the strength to leave for good. Don't be afraid.

When you're by yourself, you're not alone even when you choose to feel lonely. Only in solitude can you dive deep into yourself the same way you did with your favorite subject matter in school.

Therefore, I hope you are ready to plunge into your journey of building a new and healthy relationship with yourself.

Your core beliefs are your first superpower. When we're born, we're clean slates. We see magic all around us; we absorb words, ideas, and life experiences that, over time, build our identity.

The first seven years of our lives create the mold for the adults we're going to become. How our parents interact with us shapes our future interactions with the men and women in our lives. The dynamics between our parents, embedded in our subconscious, will impact the dynamics in our couple relationships. When we don't like what we see, we will do our best to not replicate it even if that means shutting off our hearts to love. However, when we do like what we see, we will try to mimic it. We don't really make choices based on who we are and our soul's blueprint. We try to escape or copy a model that made an impression on us as children. As a reputed psychologist once said, in most cases, when a man and a woman go to bed at night, that space gets crowded with six people: the couple and their parents.

Early in our childhoods, we acquire the bulk of our core beliefs about life, love, and who we are. Later in life, we attract events and people who match those beliefs. The only way to change what we experience on a day-to-day basis is to change our beliefs.

Some of them are buried so deep, we don't even realize we have them. However, our beliefs work in the background 24/7.

Some of the most common limiting beliefs are related to self-worth and value. Because of their childhood experiences, many people believe they are unworthy, unlovable, not good enough, not beautiful enough, or not smart enough. They rely on other people's appreciation and validation to counteract these demeaning assumptions. When the appreciation and validation go away, they feel like helm-less ships lost in raging waters.

Other limiting beliefs can be related to love, commitment, or relationships. Some people believe that true love is hard to find or that marriage is obsolete.

For many years, I equated marriage to a prison that would prevent me from fulfilling my life purpose. Somehow, I acquired the belief that any kind of committed relationship would lead to monotony, boredom, and stagnation. Inevitably, I attracted the type of partners who were unsuitable for me, or whenever things led to a future together, I would get cold feet and leave.

Limiting beliefs about the opposite gender play a part in determining what your relationship becomes. A woman who believes that "all men cheat," "all men are pigs," or "all men want just sex" will have a hard time finding a partner who loves and adores her.

Your authentic self shines beyond your limiting beliefs. Therefore, you must identify and replace them with new, empowering beliefs that reflect who you really are and the new life you want to create.

Start by identifying the limiting beliefs about yourself. Then look at your life and see if they have a real foundation.

Chances are, they don't. What's more, always remember that you have the power to transform your life and act differently right now. Imagine you are like a river that is changing all the time.

You can use different tools to nurture your new beliefs. Do it yourself by using the meditation and positive affirmations techniques presented in the previous chapter. Ask for the help of a therapist; hypnosis, the Silva Method, and even Reiki work very well.

Next, spot your limiting beliefs about the gender you're dating, relationships, and marriage. Even something as innocuous as "relationships are hard work" can play the part of the bee that moves the ox. When you bring this information into your conscious mind, you free yourself from its power. You have an opportunity to nurture new beliefs, which serve your purpose: having a happy, loving, fulfilling couple relationship. Use the same techniques as those you used for the limiting beliefs about yourself. Also, look for real-life examples of couples that thrive together, effortlessly. This will put your mind at ease because it will give your mind something tangible to work with.

Your work in terms of limiting beliefs will highlight the wounds you must heal so you can reclaim your power and authentic self.

In most cases, our parents inflict those wounds inadvertently. For example, my mother still recalls my first day at kindergarten. I know now that she loves me dearly and that she would gladly give up her life to save mine. (Yes, that's how parents are in Eastern Europe.) The three-year-old me, used to having my parents around, felt abandoned at an unfamiliar place with a bunch of strangers. When my mom picked me up early in the afternoon, my dress was still damp from the river of tears I had been crying all morning.

Lise Bourbeau explains in her excellent book, "Heal Your Wounds and Find Your True Self," that identifying the wound and going through the trauma again are important steps in the healing process. It's evident to me now that my mother didn't mean to cause me pain by registering me for kindergarten. Both my parents worked full-time as teachers, my grandma couldn't watch over me, and nannies weren't an option in communist countries.

Most people, says the author, can easily identify the primary wound but they stop here. They are afraid to relive the pain. However, this step can help you see things from a new perspective—an adult's perspective. This helps you comfort your inner child and release the old negativity stored in your cells.

As soon as I healed my abandonment trauma, my relationship with my mom and other women improved. My self-confidence skyrocketed because I fully embraced my femininity and roots and stopped being driven by the desire to not be like my mother.

If you feel any resentment or blame toward your parents, I strongly recommend that you free yourself from this burden. Forgive them for any wrong they might have done. They did the best they could in those circumstances. The harmony and peace between you and your parents will radiate its healing and loving light upon your other relationships.

Your self-confidence is your second superpower. Sometimes it feels as though whoever came up with the concept of what we experience as "Western society" had a particular purpose in mind, and undermining our self-confidence was part of it. From the moment we wake up until the moment we go to sleep, social and traditional media, advertising, and entertainment bombard us with images and ideas about who we should be, how we should act, and what we should own to be considered acceptable and successful. They make us focus on the exterior world instead of connecting with who we really are, finding and expressing our own voice. To feel worthy, we look for constant exterior validation and approval: the promotion, the bonus, the likes, the accolades, the prizes, the followers.

Often in the past, when my self-confidence ran low, I would surprise myself by bending over backward to meet other people's expectations. I put more effort into work or did something my partner expected me to do, although my heart wasn't in it at all. My lover's or boss's positive reaction would briefly boost my self-worth and self-confidence levels. But then my self-confidence tank would run empty again, and I would have to rely on the external world to re-fill it.

Eventually, I realized that self-confidence is an inside job. Real self-esteem comes from within.

When your self-worth depends on replicating somebody else's life and personality and other people's opinions, your self-confidence has the durability of a sandcastle. A gust of wind or even a gentle wave can tear it down. The water will continue to eat away at it until it becomes a flat surface. That's what a toxic partner does to your self-esteem. His behavior, whether it's belittling or taking you a guilt trip, makes you doubt yourself and your abilities. Isn't it funny how one person can have such a massive impact on you despite what everybody else is saying? As if you didn't have your hands full already, your inner critic makes the situation worse while your soul urges you to take action.

As impossible as it may seem, you must go from below-sea-level self-confidence to at least a small-hill level. Your newly regained self-confidence will help you cope with your current situation and, eventually, find a way out.

Don't run to your best friend. Take your time before hiring a therapist. And especially don't try to accommodate other people's requests or demands. Don't pretend you're a kid who must satisfy her parents.

The way out is to minimize the damage your toxic partner does to your life by reducing his importance. You can't force yourself to not care about him or what he's saying but you can build your inner strength and work on regaining self-confidence.

You can use a powerful NLP tool based on visualization. Imagine you have a volume button that you can turn down each time your partner belittles, berates, or criticizes you.

But what you really need to do is to reconnect with yourself. Remember who you are, your authentic self, and ask yourself a couple of essential questions.

What are my real values?
What is my life purpose?
What brings me joy?
What do I stand for?
What makes my heart sing?
How would my life look like if I had all the money in the world and didn't have to work a single day?
What qualities do I appreciate in myself?

Remember the challenging situations you faced and the adversities you overcame. The moments when you succeeded, mattered, or changed somebody's life for the better. They have nothing to do with what other people say. Rather, they involve whatever brings peace and contentment to your soul.

Once you become aware of who you really are—beyond your body, your social status, the money in your bank account, your job title—and know your abilities, skills, and talents, you awaken from the deep slumber of pretending to be someone you're not.

You stop pretending you're a victim or helpless or unattractive or dumb or unworthy or terrible.

The more you show up in the world as who you really are, the more self-confident you become. That's because you walk right through your fear of what other people may say, think, or do. People are too engulfed in their small worlds to really care or notice what's happening around them.

Your self-confidence levels up because you're no longer torn between who you really are, who you pretend to be, and who others want you to be. Your thoughts, words, and actions match. An enormous amount of energy is suddenly available for you to use in a creative way to make your life amazing. You're no longer walking in the dark; you know what you're capable of doing and you trust in your ability to do it. You can clearly see the right path opening in front of you.

You empower yourself to give to yourself the approval you seek from others. When you do, nobody can rock your boat. Your moments of doubting yourself or losing it get sparser and shorter. They're no longer dreadful and undermining experiences but, rather, opportunities to grow and evolve. Nobody can manipulate you anymore because your spirit is free.

Please remember that, although miracles are possible, transformation requires time. Just like a seed, your self-confidence needs time to blossom into a healthy and strong offspring. Be gentle with it and with yourself. Rejoice in every sign, no matter how small or big, of its growth. Not taking your partner's words to heart, becoming more assertive, setting healthy boundaries, acting according to your values and principles, and applying for the job of your dreams are all acts that signal progress.

However, you must take one more step to ensure that your metamorphosis into the exquisite real you reaches completion and that your cup is always full.

Your third superpower is love. So, give yourself plenty of it. Now that you've shed your old limiting beliefs and your self-confidence is going through the roof, don't you feel much better in your skin? Don't you actually like the person who gazes back at you in the mirror?

Well, maybe not entirely yet. You still notice things that are a far cry from perfection.

Maybe you don't have the body of a model on the cover of a glossy magazine, your favorite Instagram yoga influencer, or the lead actress in a superhero movie. Maybe your hair is straight and you want it to be curly, or you want the flawless white skin of royalty instead of your dark complexion and freckled cheeks. Maybe you enviously look at the teenage girls blossoming into women, wishing you could feel comfortable wearing shorts and cropped tops again.

Maybe you don't have a glamorous job like your best friend does. You still drive your old Prius while your neighbor has upgraded to a Mercedes.

Maybe you don't see yourself as the smartest person in the world. You stay away from the spotlight at parties.

And then come the other people. Those who see the world, and other people, through their narrow window of limitation. Those who like to put down other people, who have a hard time seeing someone they know succeed because that makes them feel bad about themselves. They also fear that they will lose control over you.

Their voice and your voice combined portray you as a person unworthy of love.

Also, when you ignore the whispers of your heart and the voice of your soul, you feel guilty and unworthy of love.

We're never out of words when it comes to listing our shortcomings and failures. That's how we stay stuck in our little islands of comfort, feeling miserable yet safe and secure.

If we didn't, we would have to go out into the world, shine our light, trust life, get out of the comfort zone, and transform every day. We must face our fear of failure or, as Tony Robbins says, our fear of success. We would become visible to the whole world, we would make an impact, we would become fully responsible for our actions, we would consciously create our lives. We would become powerful beyond measure ... if only we loved ourselves.

People who love themselves aren't selfish. On the contrary, they are the most loving and generous beings on the planet. Their inner cup is always full, so they still have something to offer others. They are compassionate, tolerant, empathetic, and non-judgmental.

Self-love begins with self-acceptance. Embrace who you are in this very moment and cut yourself some slack. Acknowledge that at every given moment, you're doing the best you can.

Accept your fantastic body, your primary home on this journey called life. Look in wonder at its ability to heal itself, experience all types of sensations, function without your even having to think about it. Embrace the shape of your breasts, the roundness of your hips, the shape of your nose. These are all attributes that make you unique. Unique is beautiful and sexy.

Say "thank you" to your mind—an instrument more powerful than all the computers in the world put together. Stretch it by giving it quality food every day, by learning something new and going to a new place. Nourish it with positive thoughts and affirmations.

Appreciate your heart, so loving, kind, generous, and wise. Visit her often and let her guide you and help you make the best decisions. Commune with your soul so that you stay on the right track and never forget your life purpose.

You can start your journey of self-love in many ways. You can hold a ceremony in which you declare your intention of honoring and loving yourself. Nobody else needs to be present, but you can invite your best friend and take this journey together if this keeps you accountable.

We so often focus on what's wrong with us that we forget about our greatness and our small daily accomplishments. We dream about our next significant achievement and we forget that every step we take is already a major accomplishment. Start a self-love journal in which you write daily about why you should love yourself more that day. Maybe you solved a difficult problem at work or helped somebody in need or lost one more pound.

Make a list of all the things you love about yourself. Think about your body, mind, heart, personality, skills, and talents. You'll be amazed at how you tend to overlook this stuff and at how long your list is.

Make a list of all the words of praise and appreciation other people say about you. Again, this applies to all the aspects of your being.

Make a list of your accomplishments and success. Start with your childhood and look at everything—winning a singing competition, passing the driver's license exam without making any mistakes, winning a new client for your company, being financially independent.

The last list I suggest you make is that of your flaws. Look at them with acceptance and love. Maybe some of them aren't flaws at all. Speaking your mind, for example, is an excellent way of making people trust you. Maybe others have a silver lining, a bright side that you can use to better your life and help other people.

Last but not least, to love yourself, you must stay true to yourself. When you finally stop living other's people lives and trying to please everyone, you can be true to who you are.

You are loving, beautiful, compassionate, intelligent, wise, and powerful beyond measure. You can accomplish anything you want. All the answers and guidance wait deep inside you, in your heart and soul.

When you love yourself, you reach the ultimate level of freedom because you stay true to who you are, no matter what. When you love yourself, you become invisible to toxic partners. You graduate to a superior level of life mastery—a level where this type of person has nothing more to teach you.

Your fourth superpower is self-care. Give yourself emotional, mental, and physical care.

Louise Hay's international bestseller "You Can Change Your Life" did, in fact, change my life. I am one of the millions of people on this planet whom she helped tune into the power of positive affirmations. Her book also helped me release the burden of guilt associated with taking care of myself.

I remember the day before the beginning of my first elementary school year. Dressed in my cute uniform (a light-blue knee-length dress and a navy-blue apron), my red schoolbag hanging on my back and my hair combed into two braids, I grinned at my reflection in the hallway mirror, high on pride and satisfaction. I probably would have kept staring at the little girl in front of me—the one who looked and yet didn't look like me—if my mother's stern voice hadn't brought me back down to Earth.

"You're so vain. Wearing your uniform well doesn't mean you'll do well in school."

My mother doesn't recall this conversation, but I never forgot it. It remains one of my most vivid childhood memories. The six-year-old me felt terribly mistreated and wronged. She also got the idea that looking pretty and caring about it made her guilty of a deadly sin. Because I craved my mother's love and approval, I stopped looking in the mirror. I matured into a woman who continued to appreciate the beautiful things and to dress nicely, but who never put much time and effort into elaborate makeup or outfits.

It took me years of spiritual practice to realize that giving myself the attention and care I needed wasn't vain. It was an act of self-love and respect.

We have one permanent home on Earth: our fantastic bodies. We also have a powerful manifestation tool made up of our minds and emotions. We don't neglect our apartments or our beautiful homes with backyards. We make sure they look incredible and feel good, and that everything works properly. We maintain, prevent, repair, and replace. Why would we act differently when it comes to ourselves?

When you take care of your wellbeing every day, you send a signal to the Universe that you value yourself. As a result, you will attract, in your life, people who value you. You also feel good in your skin all the time.

Why do you think a new haircut or a new dress helps when you feel down? When you enjoy your reflection in the mirror, you get a boost of self-confidence that lifts your spirits. When somebody pays you a compliment or notices the upgrade, the effect doubles.

If you're like many other women (or me), when you're stressed and unhappy, you tend to binge on comfort food, lose focus on what's essential in your life, or forget about your needs. And if you haven't brought to life the superwoman within you, you probably entertain the most negative thoughts about yourself and your life. That's typical for a toxic relationship.

By taking care of yourself, you can prevent this destructive current from engulfing you.

No matter what happens in your relationship, you must ensure that you always feel great in your skin and that you enjoy being you.

You don't have to dress up to the nines and wear makeup when you're home, like a housewife in the 1950s, but make sure you like what you see. You could use your outfit as an outlet for your creativity and as a means of expressing your personality. Always wear something that makes you feel sexy and attractive—an essential pillar of your self-confidence. For example, a friend of mine always wears exquisite underwear just because it makes her feel sexy and poised.

Take care of your hair, your skin, your nails; don't avoid beauty parlors, gyms, Pilates, and massage studios. Play with perfumes and essential oils until you find the combination that embodies you.

Choose clothes that favor your body type and size and don't be afraid to add your personal touch. Even if you don't have a Kim Kardashian budget, make sure your closet has some timeless, high-value pieces that make you feel like a queen each time you wear them.

Women have an inborn desire to be and look beautiful. We enjoy turning heads, though we're too embarrassed to admit it. That's why it is so important to fulfill this desire.

Because all aspects of our being are interconnected, taking care of only the body isn't enough. I remember a scene in the TV series "Nip/Tuck" in which the wife of a plastic surgeon increased the size of her boobs to win back her husband, only to be rejected.

Although rumor has it that intelligent women scare away men, the truth is, men are drawn to a sexy mind. By sexy, I mean smart, witty, and well-rounded. When you take care of your mind, you are less likely to fall prey to negativity and negative thinking. You think clearly and can more quickly find solutions to your problems.

Stay curious, like a child, and keep learning new things about the world and life. Stay up to date on the topics you are passionate about. Use positive affirmations daily to implement new and positive ways of thinking. Have meaningful conversations with people who are smarter or more knowledgeable than you are. Read great books. Listen to podcasts and radios shows that give you food for thought. Learn a new skill that improves your life.

Once your thoughts change, your emotions change. Did you realize that behind each emotion you experience hides a thought? The more positive your thoughts, the more positive the emotions you experience.

Fortunately, this is a two-way street. Positive emotions cleanse thinking of negativity.

So, give yourself food for the soul by immersing yourself in activities you really enjoy. Watch comedies, read fun books, or go to improv and stand-up comedy shows that will have you in stitches.

Use the mindfulness techniques presented in chapter five. Spend as much time as possible not only with people who love and appreciate you but also with people who inspire you to follow your dreams and act upon your life purpose.

Building the best possible relationship with yourself is your ticket to the promised land: a happy and fulfilling couple relationship. When you love who you are, you start enjoying your own company and no longer fear being single. You're already complete, so you don't need someone else to complete you. You stop making poor choices simply because you need to fill an inner void. You realize your life has meaning and purpose regardless of your marital status. You stop seeking love outside because you've found inside. The funny thing is, although you're not looking for it anymore, you can't escape it. People are drawn to you like a magnet. People like you, whole and complete.

One of these people is your life partner: the one who potentiates your gifts, who uplifts you and inspires you to be the best version of yourself. Together, you will continue to rise in love. You will recognize him from the very beginning, and he will recognize you.

Just give yourself time and make you sure you don't fall back into the trap of your old habits and patterns.

PLAYTIME

My Superpower List

Create a list of all the qualities that make you special and unique.

1._____   11._____

2._____   12._____

3._____   13._____

4._____   14._____

5._____   15._____

6._____   16._____

7._____   17._____

8._____   18._____

9._____   19._____

10._____   20._____

Additional qualities/notes:

_____

_____

_____

_____

_____

_____

_____

_____

_____

_____

_____

_____

_____

_____

_____

_____

_____

_____

_____

_____

_____

_____

_____

_____

_____

Step 5:
How to Stay Away from the Honey Trap (and Avoid Reliving the Past)

My love for books and writing bloomed in my early childhood. It was nourished by the bedtime stories my parents read to me before I went to sleep. Every evening, I stepped into a magical world inhabited by princes and princesses, magic creatures, and animals that talked and acted very much like human beings.

The tale of the bear tricked by the fox mad quite an impression on me. During a harsh winter, the smart fox used the bear's soft spot for honey to trap him and, subsequently, feast on the limited amount of food by herself. Had the bear not been blinded by hunger, he would have noticed the red flags and avoided the trap.

Humans do the same when they live on autopilot. They are rarely present in the moment, and most of their actions and decisions are just repetitions of the past. Some details may slightly differ, just as when you take a dress to the seamstress for altering, the fabric remains the same. The mind likes to follow the path of least resistance. Therefore, even when we entertain the prospect of making a change in our lives, we take only a few sporadic steps to fulfill our goal, then fall back into our routine.

After spending months, or even years, in a toxic relationship, you must take consistent action to reach a point where you can leave your partner and remove yourself from an environment that no longer serves you. Building your inner strength and courage—something we worked on in the previous chapters— is a giant leap forward.

Once you take that leap, you must ensure you don't act like the bear in the story. Too much honey, especially at the wrong time, doesn't serve you. I guarantee that the honey will show up at your door—fresh, fruity, golden, tempting, in a beautiful crystal jar covered with an exquisite lid. That's because the Universe sometimes tests us to make sure we're ready for the next level.

Maybe your ex will show up with an armful of roses and a contrite face. Maybe you'll encounter financial challenges. Maybe you'll feel lonely. Maybe you won't know what to do with all the free time on your hands. Inevitably, you'll crave the honey. This will be temporary, I promise. Stick to your (newly acquired) guns and continue expanding the new you.

Use this opportunity to become the number one priority in your life, know yourself better, and develop new lifestyle habits that will draw in joy, happiness, and a life partner who truly loves and appreciates you. In doing so, you'll raise your vibration above negativity. When that happens, everything around you will change for the better.

We're not born to suffer and struggle. We're here to experience joy. Joy has little to do with what other people say and do; rather, it has more to do with who you are.

This is the best time in your life to finally find your passion.

Do you imagine women like Oprah, Marianne Williamson, or Beyonce getting caught in a web of self-pity and sorrow because of how their life partners behave?

They might have arguments or contradictory conversations, but they don't dwell on them because they have no time for drama. Their lives don't revolve around a man or a relationship because life holds a deeper meaning to them.

These three women know what their passion is and they follow it fiercely. They aren't willing to compromise or waste energy on things that don't matter or that would prevent them from living life to its fullest.

Why is it essential for you to find your passion and how it can change your life?

Each of us has at least one unique gift to offer the world. When finding and expressing this gift pairs up with self-love, the inner void that led us to make all our unhappy choices goes away.

Maybe you're not aware of your gift just yet. That's where what you're passionate about kicks in. You can be passionate only about something that strongly ties into your gift, something your whole being enjoys doing.

To find out what you're passionate about, think back on your childhood days. What really made you happy back then?

I used to love books but also dancing and sports and animals, particularly dogs. Although I took up writing fiction at eight, the rest came later in life. Together with my life partner, I created an online program to help couples strengthen their heart connection and communicate better based on mindfulness, fitness, and nutrition. I can also use my spiritual abilities to help both people and animals in need.

Frequently, our minds pull us in one direction and our heart in the opposite one. To complicate things even more, sometimes our bodies feel so low on energy that they can't follow either. When you find your passion, all that tension disappears. Your mind, your heart, your soul, and your body are in sync.

Another way to uncover your passion is to go deep into your heart and explore what makes it sing. What makes you forget yourself? What makes you forget to glance at your wristwatch or to check on the number of people who liked your most recent social media post?

What puts a huge smile on your face?

What could you do for hours and hours without feeling tired or bored?

What would you do even if you didn't get paid for it?

Set aside some time to answer these questions. You'll be amazed at the answers you get. Just by contemplating them, you'll receive an inflow of energy and enthusiasm that will raise your vibration to a place that your ex or the negativity in your toxic relationship can't touch. Close your eyes and imagine how your everyday life would look, feel, taste, and sound if you chose to build it, starting from what you're passionate about.

Because the brain likes the path of least resistance, it automatically fires the old neuronal pathways. So, though you may have a hard time coming up with answers to your question, don't give up. The answers will come because the genius spark within you is eager to come to life.

Even if you feel as though you're not really passionate about something, you will eventually find it. And if you think you're too old for it, I have good news: You're not!

It's never too late to find and live your life passion. One of the most famous painters in the world, Paul Gauguin, gave up a successful career as a stockbroker and his bourgeois life in his 50s to become a full-time painter. Thinking that you're too old to find and follow your passion is nothing more than a trick the mind plays on you to keep itself in a place that's familiar and, therefore, safe.

In her book, "How to Heal Your Life," Louise Hay tells the story of a woman who enjoyed being in front of the camera. She started a successful and lucrative career in TV commercials in her senior years.

Because society tells you that you must work hard to make money, you may feel as though seeking out your passion, let alone nurturing it, would be a waste of time. How to make a life by doing what you love isn't the topic of this book. My goal, for now, is to give you the most effective tools that will empower you to find happiness and love, help you realize that a whole new life awaits you beyond the toxic bubble of your relationship.

However, for the sake of argument, think about the women I mentioned at the beginning of this chapter. They have a massive impact on the world and live amazing lives merely by following their passions. What if you are destined to achieve similar —or greater—results?

Once you find your passion, it's time to act on it.

You're one of the (still) few people on this planet who can answer the question "What are you passionate about?" in one breath. Think about how lucky and blessed you are to be in this space. Why would you want to throw such an opportunity out the window? It would be like being handed the key to a vault jammed full of treasures and then throwing that key out the window.

Ease yourself into your passion, one step at a time. This will help you forget about the drama in your personal life. It will uplift your energy and raise your vibration. The more time you spend in a space of love, harmony, and joy, the more you'll grow into it and the lower the odds that you'll fall back into your old routines.

New paths you never dreamed of will unfold at your feet, and you'll meet new people.
Spirituality knocked at my door once I decided to follow my passion for dancing by taking ballroom dancing lessons. I guess I had to reach a point in my life where I was ready to embark on this journey and do some inner work. I remember that, although the building's location made me look out the window every other minute to check my car, I decided to stay. Not only did nothing bad happen to the vehicle or me, but I also met my first Reiki master.

If you were a sailboat on open waters, your passion would be the wind that was pushing you forward. The more time and energy you put into your passion, the more support you get from the Universe. Before you know it, your fears subside and you trust the flow of life.

Fear keeps you tied to your unhappy past and is probably the hardest anchor to break. However, fear is nothing more than energy vibrating at a very low frequency. The most efficient ways to overcome fear are to do what you fear as well as to raise your vibration and keep it high.

The good thing about getting rid of fear is that it allows you to more easily free yourself from other, smaller anchors such as habit, your comfort zone, and even addiction. Your mind can finally focus on positive things and listen to the whisper of your heart.

So, ask yourself: How can you follow your passion? You don't have to replicate what other people are doing; just stay true to yourself. Like the medicine man, Juan, beautifully puts it in Carlos Castaneda's masterpiece "The Teachings of Don Juan," all you need is to know your heart. Dive deep into it, just as you'd jump into the turquoise pool of water formed where rapids charge into the soil. Then, allow the answer to come to you.

Maybe you need to take a dance class like I did, or perhaps you want to go back to school and get a master's degree or Ph.D. Maybe all you need is to take an online course, attend a couple of workshops, or read a few books. One of my favorite aerobic classes is taught by a lady who is 65. She's simply amazing at her job, always smiling and full of positive energy. She told me she became a fitness instructor in her early 40s because she was already spending a lot of time at the gym being passionate about fitness and healthy living.

Perhaps you just need to open a new blank document on your computer and start typing. Or buy some brushes, colors, and canvas. Set up your own blog where you share your amazing vegan recipes or your poems.

Don't think for a second about how many people are already doing it, or how good they are at it. Don't be embarrassed or ashamed. Don't doubt your potential and ability. If you open the right door, people will find you and everything will miraculously unfold. Don't bend your ear to the naysayers, to the people who doubt everyone and everything.

Be like the sun casting its light freely because that's his nature. Rejoice in remembering your life passion. I use the word "remember" because I know that your passion has always been there. You were just too busy and out of sync with yourself to pay any attention to it.

This is precisely your goal now: to remember and express your true nature. Sometimes, at the very beginning, we don't have to know the whole plan. Elon Musk had no idea what impact he'd make in the world when he started his first business based on his passion for video games. That didn't prevent him from becoming a thought leader in our modern world. He simply followed his heart and intuition.

Each new step you take along your passion path reveals a bit more of the bigger plan. Then, at one point, you'll look behind yourself and marvel at how far you've come. At that point, you'll realize that time and life are too precious to waste on petty quarrels or people indulging themselves in a place of negativity and stagnation.

Whether it's your passion or anything else in life, always listen to your intuition. This whisper of your soul never betrays you, never tricks you, and always aims to serve your highest good. It always ensures you are on the path of least resistance. Some spiritual teachers say we always end up where we're supposed to be. However, our inner guide smoothens our journey and keeps us away from unnecessary delays.

True love, joy, and abundance can be found at any age, but why not accept these gifts and reclaim our birthright early in life?

Your passion will show you how to allow yourself to receive these gifts. Then, before you know it, you will have your a-ha moment. You will find yourself living your life purpose.

*

*   *

Your passion guides you to your life purpose.

Now that you know your passion, don't you feel elated, empowered, and more self-confident? Your life suddenly and subtly has more meaning. Your passion energizes you; it's something you want to explore, to dwell on, to become an essential part of your life. No wonder! Your passion leads you to your life purpose.

I can't say this enough: Only self-love and living your life purpose can fill your inner emptiness and add meaning to your life. All the rest is distraction and delusion. That's why living your life purpose is such a powerful tool to prevent you from falling back into your old patterns.

When you're in a toxic relationship, it is hard to think about your life purpose. Or even when you know it, it's almost impossible to live it because you are swimming in a sea of negativity. The two can't coexist in the same space and time, just as love and fear can't exist side-by-side.

When you live your life purpose, everything falls into place. You are in the right place, at the right time, meeting the right people, including your life partner.

Nancy Rivard, founder of the successful non-profit Airline Ambassadors International and a beautiful soul whom I'm honored to call my friend, knew her life mission—to bring love into action—since early childhood. By sticking to her life purpose despite challenges, betrayals, and hardships, she has saved millions of lives, including victims of human trafficking. She also met the love of her life, her husband, Dave Rivard. Her life story is a lesson in love, grit, and courage, and she shares it in her memoir, "Wings of Love."

Even if you're strong, temptations will appear along the way. In all likelihood, you won't be able to maintain your focus 24/7, at least not in the beginning.

It took me a while to nestle myself comfortably into my life purpose and to allow nothing or no one to pull me out. Before that, my toxic relationships always took a toll on my ability to focus on my life purpose. Words and actions would scratch old wounds and bruise my ego. I ended up in a circle, repeating old patterns again and again. At some point, I had to consciously choose to live my life purpose as the number one priority in my life.

This allowed me to stay in a loving and positive space that impacted all the aspects of my life.

We are energy, connected to each other and everything else that exists in the Universe. Our first interaction with another being happens at a subtle energy level. In those very first seconds, we unconsciously pick up all the information we need to know. If our energies match, we feel at ease and like that person. If they don't, we might experience discomfort and dislike.

We are also connected to the subconscious field of energy of humankind. Sometimes, our thoughts, feelings, or emotions may not even belong to us; we simply borrow them from somebody else.

Imagine what happens when you live under the same roof or interact daily with a person who is full of negativity or who is manipulating or belittling you.

By holding your space and staying in a loving vibration, you prevent other people's energy from negatively affecting you. The more you stay there and cultivate that energy, the more it builds up. When it gets strong enough, you can change the energy around you for the better simply by walking into a room. Think for a moment about your life when, let's say, you were in a stormy work meeting and everybody calmed down when a confident person walked into the room. Or, if you like going to spiritual centers, think about how you feel when you step inside.

I remember moderating a panel on self-publishing versus traditional publishing at a writers' conference in LA. At one point, the dialogue between the panelists got as heated as a presidential debate. All ended well, and the speakers left the room on friendly terms. The fiercest of them thanked me for bringing peace to the table and keeping things under control. I didn't yell or slam my fist on the table. I just held my space and the inner intention that the workshop provides the best experience and information for all involved.

Living your life purpose gives you the wings you need to fly high above the angry ocean or burning fields. It isn't something you do or undertake every now and then. It is an essential part of your life, the same as breathing and eating.

On some days, you will take specific actions related to your life purpose. On other days, you will simply visualize it and listen to your heart to know what you need to do next. Sometimes, you'll hear "go, it's time," while at other times, the same voice will tell you to wait, be, and enjoy the present moment.

Your life purpose will grow and evolve with you. At some point, you might even discover that you have more than one life purpose. For example, every 10 years, my dear friend Mike chose to explore a different gift of his and turn it into a life purpose.

Stability and predictability serve us in moderation. They're right when they help us meet our basic needs and count on our life partner or boyfriend. But this doesn't really happen in a toxic relationship, does it? Otherwise, they become a self-imposed prison where we forget about our awesomeness and turn into robots with dead stares.

Ultimately, your life purpose helps you stay alive and young and enjoy life to the fullest despite the passing of the years. Did you notice that senior people who lead fulfilling lives are more energetic than people in their 20s or 30s?

Ultimately, following your life purpose is about having a positive impact on the world. It can be about touching the lives of those around you in a meaningful way or leaving a legacy that will endure the test of time and elevate future generations.

In the Universal tapestry of creation, there is no such thing as a small or big purpose. Don't mistake fame, wealth, or social status for life purpose. These can show up in your life as byproducts. Because we're all connected, even the smallest act of kindnesses has a ripple effect.

As long as your heart sings, you're fulfilling your destiny.

*

*   *

If your life were a home, by now it would look and feel bright and tidy. Dwelling in it would give you tremendous pleasure. Think about how far you've traveled and how much you've grown—from a person caught up in the web of a toxic relationship to someone who greets every day with a smile on her face because she loves herself and knows and lives her life purpose. However, it's worth taking one more look and sweeping away any cobwebs you might have missed in the dark corners, to make sure they won't invade your house again.

The cobwebs consist of seemingly harmless and insignificant details that can build up and drag you back into your old world of sorrow and suffering.

An important step is to reduce, to a minimum, the time you spend with your toxic partner. Even if you're still together or living under the same roof until you feel ready to leave, try to be outside his reach as much as possible. Find something to do, someplace to be, away from him. If you're a busy professional, this shouldn't be too hard.

If you're a mother, you're going to do your kids a favor by removing them from a toxic environment. Kids quickly pick up on the vibes around them and also internalize the models of the relationships they see between their parents or the grown-ups around them. A toxic environment will have a negative impact later in life, influencing their mindset and behavior.

Once you decide to distance yourself from your toxic partner, and once he senses that he has lost you, he might refuse to let you go. Don't let yourself be intimidated by threats and don't give in to promises. When they want something, people can go above and beyond, including changing their behavior to match your needs and expectations. Although I don't recommend living in the past, this is an excellent moment to look at your history. It will help you see the pattern and keep you away from the trap.

Another good strategy to prevent yourself from falling back into your old ways is to imagine what your life would be like in one, five, or ten years if you stayed in your toxic relationship. Would you be happy and feel fulfilled? Or would you be bitter and resentful? Would you do the things you like to do, or would you be stuck in a boring routine? Would you enjoy the company of your friends and family, or would you have no one to talk to because your toxic partner pushed away your dear ones?

Keep in mind that your relationship affects your health, too. For example, people who harbor resentment and unforgiveness can develop cancer at some point in their lives. Too much stress can cause your hair to turn gray prematurely. A lack of energy in your body will make you feel tired and confused.

However, I'm not an advocate of the idea that people never change. People change when they really want to change because they have a strong internal motivation to do so. They reach a point in their lives where they want to explore who they really are. Your heart will easily recognize this type of person. They will continue to walk their (new) talk even if you turn them down. That's because they have changed not to impress or manipulate somebody but, rather, because they felt the need to do so.

Also, a relationship may have moments of toxicity, especially in the beginning, without being entirely toxic. The two partners purge old patterns, wounds, beliefs, and limitations. They learn how to coexist, to open their hearts to love and another person.

During the first few months of my current relationship, my partner and I fought a lot. We started out as friends, and I swore that he was the kindest, most loving man in the world. However, as we got closer and our friendship turned into something more profound, the ghosts of the past showed their ugly faces. Not a week would go by without us having a massive argument, which depleted us of energy and joy. However, neither of us walked away. Instead, we sat down and talked. We made lists, talked about our feelings and emotions, and came up with actionable steps that would help us prevent or appease our future crises.

"What's the point in going through all these fights if we don' t learn anything?" he would ask.

Our relationship changed from a battlefield to an oasis of peace and love, where we genuinely support and care about each other. In retrospect, I believe all the turmoil was worth it. It helped us grow and learn a few lessons, which otherwise the next partner would have taught us. Universal laws ensure that the same experiences pop up in our lives again and again until we learn our lessons from them.

So, don't rush into decisions and actions. If you do, it could be your auto-pilot kicking in. By now, you don't want that to happen anymore. You want to be aware of your thoughts, words, and deeds.

Take the necessary time for reflection and especially for connecting with your heart and soul. Listen to their guidance. Always follow the whisper of your intuition.

Let your intuition show you the ideal relationship for you. Close your eyes and imagine how it would be. Visualize the activities you would do with your partner, your conversations, what a Sunday together would look like. Feel loved, cherished, spoiled, treated like a queen. Experience what it's like to be the most important person in someone's life. Imagine a life filled with joy, happiness, wellbeing, adventure, fun, sensuality, love, wealth, and passion.

If this picture doesn't meet your needs and desires, feel free to change it accordingly. I simply can't imagine that any woman would want to live a different life, one in which she is abused, mistreated, and taken for granted.

PLAYTIME

I am passionate about:

_____

_____

_____

_____

_____

_____

_____

_____

_____

_____

Steps I need to take to follow my passion:

_____

_____

_____

_____

_____

_____

_____

_____

_____

_____

_____

My life purpose is to

_____

_____

_____

_____

_____

_____

_____

_____

_____

_____

Step 6:
Say Adios to All Relationship-Induced
Toxicity in Your Life

If toxicity pesters your couple relationship, it most likely manifests itself in other areas of your life, too. Please remember that, no matter what other people say (including those you hold in high esteem), you are entitled to live a happy, rewarding, and loving life. The fact that you can't and don't want to please everybody, and that you have clear priorities in your life, doesn't make you an evil or selfish person.

In other types of relationships, toxicity may manifest as manipulation, belittling, guilt trips, or withdrawal of affection. Different people who are close to you can consciously or unconsciously act like that in an attempt to have things their way, control you, or satisfy their needs.

People can have a hard time seeing other people succeed, as they fear being left behind. Or perhaps they simply want to protect you and act upon their life experience and expectations. Even when their intentions stem from a place of genuine care, their behavior doesn't serve you.

Look at the other meaningful relationships in your life and run a toxicity check-up. The other person can be a parent, your best friend, a sibling, a co-worker, or your boss.

Ask yourself:

How does this relationship make me feel?

Does this relationship support my aspirations, my goals, my dreams?

How do I feel when I'm around this person? How do I feel after we part?

Do I feel comfortable being authentic and expressing myself freely in this relationship?

Tudor was a handsome, successful attorney when I met him. His demeanor and style made his single female co-workers fantasize about him. They imagined he lived in a palace and they wondered what the most important woman in his life was like.

That woman had some grays. She was also small and frail. The woman was his mother. Every Friday afternoon, Tudor jumped in his car and drove about 150 miles to see her. She always waited for him with his favorite meals on the table. She also never missed an opportunity to complain about the time and effort she had put into cooking that meal. How hard it was for a woman her age to do it all by herself. Her husband, Tudor's father, had passed away when his son was five and she had never remarried.

Tudor felt a lump in his throat and clenched his fists. After all, he never asked for anything. He also remembered the many times when he had to cancel plans, such as taking a trip with his ex-girlfriend, because his mother suddenly felt sick.

Although young, Tudor walked like an old man, his hands interlaced behind his back. He always stuck to the same routine when he visited his mother and he rarely smiled.

Fast forward to 10 years later; Tudor is still single and goes to see his mom every weekend.

Tudor's story is a classic example of a toxic relationship between a child and his parent. Out of fear of being alone, his mother inadvertently, yet regularly, played the victim so she could have Tudor's undivided attention. She left no room for another woman in his son's life, and he accepted that fact.

Don't get me wrong. Our parents do the best they can and have our best interests at heart. But they're human, too, and most of the time they're unaware of the subconscious destructive forces that drive their actions. Sometimes, some kind of fear hides behind their attention.

Your parents gave you life. They fed you, gave you an education, and put a roof over your head. But that doesn't mean they own you or can dictate how you should live your life. You don't have to fulfill their unfulfilled dreams if that isn't your goal. You don't have to adopt a particular lifestyle to express your gratitude. You certainly don't have to give up your dreams just to show you're a good daughter or son.

Treat your parents with respect and show them love, but don't allow them to manipulate you into not listening to your heart. Remember: Although they still see you as a child, you're a grown-up fully capable of making the best decisions.

You can't force your parents to change; that's a sure thing. However, as you grow and evolve internally, your relationship with your parents will automatically change. When you do the inner work, you free them of the role they had to play in your life. Abusive fathers who never knew how to express their feelings become best friends. Mothers who were unable to communicate with their daughters, who were overly criticizing and demanding, suddenly become the most active fans of their daughters.

I tell you from experience that accepting and loving your parents unconditionally is one of the most elating feelings in the world. When you do, you finally embrace who you are. To reach that point, you may need to step away for a while. Gather the strength and knowledge necessary to hold a loving space for both of you. It's almost impossible to have a healthy couple relationship until you make peace with your parents.

*

*   *

The person you see as your best friend can sometimes be the most toxic presence in your life. This usually happens when one of you makes progress in different life areas while the other remains stuck.

The one who is stuck will do anything to prevent the other person from moving on with their life.

Although I'm not proud of this story, I will share it with you to make my point.

Marius and I had an instant connection and we became the best friends in the world in no time. I would call him my "brother from another mother," and I would be his sister. As we were both single, we spent most of our free time together and we did a ton of fun stuff. Marius always sang my praises; to him, I was a sort of goddess on a pedestal: beautiful, intelligent, kind, and nurturing. Whenever I felt sad or disappointed, his was the shoulder I cried on. He would have jumped in his car and driven over at 3 a.m. if I needed him because I was the priority in his life.

A year and a half into our friendship, Marius met an adorable young woman. Both of us had made attempts at dating, but nothing was serious. This time, it was different because she was special and showed him the unconditional love that nobody had ever given him.

Marius' eyes glittered with joy each time he talked about her. As their relationship progressed, he reassured me that I still had the most important place in his heart.

Instead of supporting his budding relationship and feeling happy for him, I felt betrayed and jealous. I started acting on those feelings. I played the victim, the forsaken friend. I declined his calls, making him come to my door. I did all kinds of crazy stuff, which I deeply regret.

When I finally woke up to what I was doing, it was too late. Marius had wisely chosen his relationship over our one-way friendship. He had done the hard work; I had played the role of the happy recipient.

Friendship is a two-way street. Your best friend will always rejoice in your success, happiness, and joy. They will support you through hardships and do nothing to hinder your wellbeing. They will show understanding, tolerance, and compassion. They will help you grow and nurture your relationship with your significant other or your dreams. They won't be jealous or envious of you and the good in your life.

They won't make you feel guilty for doing well in life.

They won't make you give up what you love simply to prove to them how much they matter to you.

They won't throw a tantrum when you don't do what they want.

On the flip side...

A good friend will keep his promises. He won't keep you hanging, waiting for an answer or a call. He won't bail on you minutes before the movie starts unless he has an excellent reason to do so.

A good friend will help you without expecting anything in return or making a fuss over it.

A good friend will wipe your tears without saying, "I told you so."

A good friend will call you just to check on you.

A good friend will make time for you and will meet you in person.

A good friend will be your friend regardless of where he is in the world.

A good friend will always tell you the truth, even if it hurts.

A good friend won't judge you.

When we realize that not all relationships are meant to last a lifetime, we find it easier to let go of people who clearly don't belong in our lives anymore. We can part ways peacefully, at least on our end, and appreciate all the good, the growth, the lessons these people brought into our lives.

Instead of building thick walls of sorrow and disappointment around hearts, we swing the door wide open for more good and beautiful people to enter our lives. I find the idea that long-lasting friendships are forged during childhood to be dated. As more and more people awaken, more of us connect at a heart level. When we nourish these instant connections, we create amazing, long-lasting friendships, no matter how young or old we are. Love and understanding flow unhindered between our friends and us, creating an unbreakable bond.

*

* *

Most people I know have full-time jobs. They have told me many stories about how a toxic work environment or colleague ruined their day and drained them.

Vince is a caring, generous, creative man who lives in Dublin, Ireland. He would enjoy his job as a public servant if it weren't for his boss, Tim, who continually finds fault with Vince. Ordinarily gregarious and self-assured, Vince is always out of words in front of his superior. After each confrontation, which usually happens in front of co-workers, Vince feels like a crushed bug. His levels of self-confidence, self-worth, and self-esteem plummet like stocks on a bad day. It takes him days to recover and become the joyful Vince everybody loves, only to be put down again.

When dealing with a toxic co-worker or boss or even a neighbor, you have only two options: get a new job or a new place, or look for the lesson, learn it, and pass the test.

The first solution will work in the short term. The second one will work for the long term and will free you from negativity.

When talking to Vince about his life, I realized that the root of his problem lay in his childhood. Although he's not Jewish, when he was a few years old, his parents decided to take him to the doctor's office and have him circumcised. They didn't ask for his opinion. They just felt it would be best for his health, but they didn't take the time to explain to him why.

Five-year-old Vince felt betrayed, abused, less of a man, embarrassed, ashamed. He thought that he must have done something terrible for his parents to inflict such a punishment on him. His self-esteem and self-worth took a hard blow that still affects him.

When I told him that I had been in a relationship with a circumcised without minding it, he acted surprised. "I thought girls hate it," he confessed.

I explained to Vince that he shouldn't build resentment against his boss; on the contrary, he should show gratitude. The man was bringing to the surface an old wound that needed healing. He was allowing my friend to release his old beliefs that he wasn't worthy or man enough. As soon as Vince did that, the boss would change his behavior, be moved to another department, or transfer to another company.

While you do your inner work, don't let the toxic people at work get to you. Remember: You have no control over the circumstances of the outer world, but you can always choose how you respond to them.

Don't take anything personally. Unhappy people are usually aggressive and morose.

Find at least one good quality in the most annoying person.

Greet everyone with a smile.

Don't fight back and retaliate. Refuse to get into a battle of the egos. Instead, be assertive and clearly express your point of view.

Also, always do your best to keep a track record of your accomplishments and successes.

If you are employed full-time, you must create and maintain a pleasant environment at work. Otherwise, your experience at work will affect the other aspects of your life, the same way your toxic relationship takes a toll on your work performance. When you return home, leave all tension and frustration at your doorstep. Don't take it inside to your partner or dear ones.

All your efforts and changes will pay off in time, maybe even sooner than you expect.

PLAYTIME

Friends I love to be around:

_____
_____
_____
_____
_____

Friends who wear me out:

_____
_____
_____
_____
_____

Things I love about my mom:

_____
_____
_____
_____

Things I love about my dad:

_____
_____
_____
_____

Things I like about my favorite co-worker:

_____

_____

_____

_____

I dislike _____ from work because

_____

_____

_____

__. However, I appreciate her/him for _____

_____

_____

_____

_____

_____

Super - Diane's Gift

As I beamed with excitement like the summer sun, I allowed the words to burst out of my mouth:

"I'm writing a book on toxic relationships!"

Mike shook his head, his eyes sparkling.

"I don't believe in such a thing as a toxic relationship, but sure, if that's what you want..."

There was no trace of judgment or scolding in his voice. He had simply voiced his heart. Mike made me think that maybe one of the reasons he has such a loving and harmonious relationship with Ai was because he did not believe in the existence of toxic relationships. I realized I don't get to experience things I never think about (such as disease or aging) because they're not part of my belief system. If you're going to examine your life, you will notice that you always end up experiencing what you fear the most. You cringe when you see a police car; inevitably, the highway patrol will pull you over for speeding. You fear your partner will cheat on you; an incriminatory text pops up on their cell screen. You fear traffic will be terrible during the holidays ... and that's what you get because that's what you order.

Mike also made me think about the way we experience life by labeling people, places, and experiences, and about how much richer our existence would be if we didn't try to make it fit inside the tiny box of our limited perception. For example, instead of labeling a rainy day as a bad day, you could take it in with all your senses. Feel the water caressing your skin; inhale the fresh, humid scent; listen to the steady, soothing drumming of the drops on rooftops and sidewalks; count the nuances of gray in the sky. When you're caught in traffic, you could look at the other drivers, maybe roll down your window, give them a smile, and say, "Hello, how is your day?"

This sounds crazy, right? You grew up just like I did, believing that everybody outside your family and friends is a stranger. And you're not supposed to talk to strangers. You're not supposed to care about strangers. Strangers can be dangerous.

You were brought up to believe you're separate from everybody else. That your being ends where your skin ends. Nobody told you that you have an energy body that spreads out a few good feet around you. Nobody told you that you're actually connected to a unified field of energy that unites everything and everyone.

You had to fight hard and use a tremendous amount of energy to be someone you're not and to keep in place the tall walls around your heart. To blame, judge, hate, be angry, be stuck.

The simple gesture of treating a stranger as a brother—because, after all, we are all brothers and sisters in the billion-member family of the human race—can free you from this burden. Although other people, including your dear ones, may label you as a lunatic at first, they will end up following in your footsteps. At least some of them will; the others will stay behind. You can't force them to keep up with you, nor can they hold you back unless you allow them to do so. Nobody can force you into anything, not even when they point a gun at you.

"I don't believe in toxic relationships, either," I replied to Mike. "But I do believe relationships can be toxic when we refuse to learn the lesson and indulge in pain."

"Maybe," he said wistfully.

Maybe we need to experience pain for a while to have contrast in our lives, so we can better appreciate the good.

Eventually, all pain comes to an end and life changes for the better. Whenever and wherever there is an excess of polarized energy, positive or negative, the Universe steps in to restore balance and harmony.

As a teenager, I used to listen to Diane on the radio. She was one of my favorite DJs because of her husky voice and rock music playlist. She also looked like a rock star, with long blonde hair and a slender body. Even after I became a radio host with the same station, I still looked up to her ... until the summer when she almost begged me to be her guest at the seaside. I had thought she was invincible. Untouchable.

Diane had a master's degree in Language and Literature. She hosted a popular night talk show and always spoke her mind. She called the top musicians in our city by their first names. She always got the men she wanted. She appeared to know everything. She knew the answer to every question, especially when it came to topics such as culture, music, politics, and society. Assertive and self-confident, she looked down on some people, especially pretty women. At 18, I thought someone of her status and value was supposed to behave like that. We never interacted much, and we certainly didn't become friends.

But that summer, when she heard I was at the seaside, she invited me over. By then, both of us had transitioned to other jobs. I was a TV host and producer while she was an A&R manager for a record company.

Back then, I still believed that my body was just a bag of flesh and bones. I had no clue about energy or energy work or how other people or surrounding energy could affect me. However, the moment we met, I felt an urge to leave.

The all-powerful Diane had morphed into a meek, vulnerable creature. She also looked shorter than I remembered. Finally out of a draining seven-year relationship, she felt lonely and needed some company.

She confessed that the relationship had slowly and steadily broken her like Chinese drop torture. Diane's partner had identified her soft spots and used them to rob her of her self-confidence, self-esteem, and self-worth. He had abused her emotionally and physically. He had made her fear leaving him by threatening to harm herself or her. He had cut her off from her friends and family.

Every time she reached the end of her rope and decided to leave him, he would change gears and tell her he couldn't live without her. Every time, she believed him and stayed.

Seven years went by in the blink of an eye. Diane's health started deteriorating. Her back hurt day and night and she had weekly migraines, forcing her to take long medical leaves that almost cost her her job.

One day, she looked into the mirror and shrieked in horror. She was in her late 30s, but her reflection looked like that of a 50-

year-old. Her partner had also gotten into drinking, becoming more violent than before. She decided to leave him before she completely lost herself or her life.

I didn't ask Diane why she had opened her heart to me. Maybe her experience had endowed her with the sort of wisdom that allows one to read other people, beyond what they say and do. Perhaps she had sensed that, in a way, I felt as lost as she did and was about to make the same mistakes she had made.

Maybe she had sensed that, of all the people she knew, I would be the only one who wouldn't judge her and who would keep her secret.

Maybe I was the only person who had replied to her message.

As I listened to her, I realized how Diane's experiences over the past years had dissolved her superwoman shield, making her human.

Diane told me to stay away from toxic men who would steal my freedom and my soul, leaving me doubting my ability to make decisions. She said she would have left her ex sooner if only she hadn't pushed away all her friends and behaved like a bitch with her family and other people when things were great. With a defeated look in her eyes, Diane confessed that she regretted most the years she had wasted, her early youth, which would never return. She told me again that she'd happily share her hotel room with me.

As much as I wanted to help her, I had to go. I told her I had other engagements, but I would do my best to come back for at least one day. I simply couldn't tell her the truth.

Although Diane had lost that battle, she didn't lose the war. She never got back with her ex. As time went by, she regained her strength and self-confidence. Joy and excitement returned to her life. Diane reinvented herself and started a new life in a new country. Her Facebook profile again showed pictures of the Super Diane I knew—a passionate woman, driving a sports car on a racetrack.

However, there was something else about her I had never seen before: kindness, empathy, appreciation, and support of other people. She was a Diane who had friends and who enjoyed having them visit her in her new home. I realized that if not for her toxic partner, Diane would never have experienced these feelings. She wouldn't have had the chance to touch other people's lives in a meaningful, positive way. Many people's lives would have been poorer if Diane hadn't gone through the ordeal of her toxic relationship.

In the end, the relationship she had labeled as toxic offered her the greatest gift. It opened her heart, a gift she's still paying forward.

So, what if instead of putting a label on your relationship, you decided to see and use the gift? Take this opportunity to move forward with your life. You can vacuum up all negativity by using the power of your beliefs, thoughts, words, and actions.

You can walk away from your toxic relationship in gratitude and appreciation instead of feeling abused and mistreated. You may say it's hard, that a toxic relationship eats you alive the same way cancer does. Yet, I know people who had cancer and who were cured; now they feel grateful for having been through such a life-changing experience. They say cancer broke them open, helped them realize what really matters in life. It helped them be present in the moment, love themselves, and conquer their fear of death.

Every challenging experience, including a toxic relationship, can have the same impact provided you don't dwell on it more than is necessary to learn from it.

Remember that although you're an infinite being, you have only so much time on this planet. You're meant to play and experience different emotions and situations. You have the power to decide when you've had enough of a specific experience and you get to choose a new one—one that better suits your needs or who you are at this point in your life. Or not even that. You can choose a certain experience for the sake of it.

How about you make a new choice today, one that is different from everything you've lived through lately? Why not choose to be happy, loved, loving, joyful, fulfilled? Why not choose partnership, friendship, growth, health, wellbeing?

You deserve to be with a person with whom you can rise in love, who feels like home, who will stand by your side no matter what. If you accept and embrace it, it will become manifest in your life.

Made in United States
Orlando, FL
21 January 2022

13865573R00093